CW00433778

Contents

Illustrations

Figures

The New Economics of Inequality and Redistribution

Economists warn that policies to level the economic playing field come with a hefty price tag. But this so-called "equality–efficiency trade-off" has proven difficult to document. The data suggest, instead, that the extraordinary levels of economic inequality now experienced in many economies are detrimental to the economy. Moreover, recent economic experiments and other evidence confirm that most citizens are committed to fairness and are willing to sacrifice to help those less fortunate than themselves. Incorporating the latest results from behavioral economics and the new microeconomics of credit and labor markets, Bowles shows that escalating economic disparity is not the unavoidable price of progress. Rather it is policy choice – often a very costly one. Here, drawing on his experience both as a policy advisor and an academic economist, he offers an alternative direction, a novel and optimistic account of a more just and better working economy.

Samuel Bowles heads the Behavioral Sciences Program at the Santa Fe Institute. He has taught economics at Harvard University, the University of Massachusetts, and the University of Siena. He is the author, most recently, of *Microeconomics: Behavior, Institutions, and Evolution* (2004), *A Co-operative Species: Human Reciprocity and its Evolution* (2011, with Herbert Gintis), and articles in *Science*, *Nature*, the *Quarterly Journal of Economics*, the *Journal of Public Economics*, and other academic journals. He has also served as an economic advisor to US presidential candidates Robert F. Kennedy and Jesse Jackson, and former South African President Nelson Mandela, and has taught crash courses in economics to trade unionists, community activists, and others.

Federico Caffè Lectures

This series of annual lectures was initiated to honor the memory of Federico Caffè. They are jointly sponsored by the Department of Public Economics at the University of Rome, where Caffè held a chair from 1959 to 1987, and the Bank of Italy, where he served for many years as an advisor. The publication of the lectures will provide a vehicle for leading scholars in the economics profession, and for the interested general reader, to reflect on the pressing economic and social issues of the times.

The New Economics of Inequality and Redistribution

Samuel Bowles

in collaboration with
Christina Fong, Herbert Gintis, Arjun Jayadev, and **Ugo Pagano**

CAMBRIDGE
UNIVERSITY PRESS

CAMBRIDGE
UNIVERSITY PRESS

University Printing House, Cambridge CB2 8BS, United Kingdom

Cambridge University Press is part of the University of Cambridge.

It furthers the University's mission by disseminating knowledge in the pursuit of education, learning and research at the highest international levels of excellence.

www.cambridge.org
Information on this title: www.cambridge.org/9781107601604

First published 2012
3rd printing 2014

Printed in the United Kingdom by Clays, St Ives plc

A catalog record for this publication is available from the British Library

Library of Congress Cataloging in Publication data
Bowles, Samuel.
The new economics of inequality and redistribution / Samuel Bowles in collaboration with Christina Fong, Herbert Gintis, Arjun Jayadev, and Ugo Pagano.
    pages cm. – (Federico Caffè lectures)
Includes bibliographical references and index.
ISBN 978-1-107-60160-4 (pbk.)
1. Income distribution.   2. Fairness.   I. Title.
HB523.B685   2012
339.2–dc23
                                                                    2012004203

ISBN 978-1-107-01403-9 Hardback
ISBN 978-1-107-60160-4 Paperback

For
Gerald Cohen (1941–2009) and
David Gordon (1944–1996)
in memoriam

Table

Preface

Radical egalitarianism – the dream of equal freedom – is now the orphan of a defunct socialism. The unruly and abandoned child of the liberal enlightenment had found a home in nineteenth-century democratic socialism. Protected and overshadowed by its new foster parent, radical egalitarianism was relieved of the burden of arguing its own case: as European socialism's foster child, economic and political equality would be the by-product of an unprecedented post-capitalist order, not something to be defended morally and promoted politically on its own terms in the world as it is.

It thus fell to reformists, be they laborist, social-democratic, Euro-communist or New Deal, to make capitalism livable for workers and the less well-off, a task they accomplished with remarkable success in some of the advanced economies. But in the process, the egalitarian project was purged of its utopian yearnings. Its objectives were narrowed to the pursuit of a more equal distribution of goods and formal equality of political rights. The "world turned upside down" that Gerrard Winstanley had promised as the seventeenth-century Diggers were occupying Saint George's Hill near London was not to be; workers and farmers would have to settle for a world smoothed out. Over the years even this project has encountered increasingly effective resistance and experienced major political reversals. The century-long decline in the income shares of the very rich in virtually every country on which we have adequate data came to an abrupt halt in the final quarter of the twentieth century (Atkinson, Piketty, and Saez 2011). In many of the world's largest economies – the US, the UK, India, China, and others – the economic fortunes of the very rich regained much of their lost ground.

Is egalitarianism passé? I think not. Surprisingly, two reasons to doubt the prevailing "equality pessimism" come from economics.

The first is the demise of the self-interested *Homo economicus* as the reigning behavioral model in economics, brought down by the onslaught of experimental and other evidence showing that people willingly share even when big money is at stake, and that they avidly punish those who treat others unfairly, even if they have to pay in order to do this (Bowles and Gintis 2011). The fact that large fractions of experimental subjects exhibit what are termed *social preferences* including altruism, reciprocity, and even "inequality-aversion" invites a reconsideration not only of the political feasibility of egalitarian policies but also of the economic feasibility of cooperative production and other institutional alternatives.

The second reason to question equality pessimism is a revolution in the economic theory of contracts (Stiglitz 1987, Laffont 2000). Economists have sidelined the once-conventional assumption that contracts and markets are complete, meaning that everything that is transacted in an exchange is specified in a contract that is enforceable at no cost to the exchanging parties. This seemingly technical adjustment in economic theory led inexorably to big changes in the take-home message. This is that, where it really matters, Adam Smith's invisible hand is broken: market failures are endemic to exchanges that are central to the workings of a capitalist economy – labor and credit markets. It's getting harder to treat the failures of *laissez-faire* as mere caveats to be taken up in the last week of the semester (if there is time) and illustrated by bucolic external economies like Farmer Jones' bees pollinating Farmer Bell's apple orchard or public goods like lighthouses. The big news for the economics of inequality is that, as we will see, market failures can sometimes be attenuated by an egalitarian redistribution of wealth and decision-making power.

These two new developments – the first about what people are like, the second about how people interact – have far-reaching ramifications. But surprisingly, these new economics of social preferences and incomplete contracts have not been consistently applied to the study of public policies to achieve economic security and distributional justice. *The New Economics of Inequality and Redistribution* does this. The result is a rejection of equality pessimism and an affirmation that egalitarian redistribution, if properly implemented, is not only good economics – because it can improve incentives for high-level performance in a modern economy – but also winning politics – because it embraces people's generosity and ethical commitments. If I had to do a bumper sticker for the new economics of inequality it would be: INEQUALITY: IT DOESN'T WORK AND PEOPLE DON'T LIKE IT.

The ideas that I present here did not originate in my study or in a university seminar room. For the most part they occurred to me while I was attempting to address difficult questions of economic policy and political strategy that were pressed on me either by policy-makers and political activists or by my own inability to explain the most basic economic facts that I observed around me.

By age 11 I had noticed how very average I was among my Indian classmates at the Delhi Public School – in sports, in school work, in just about everything. How does it come about, I asked my mother, that Indians are so much poorer than Americans, if we cannot run faster and calculate sums more accurately than Indians? Her reply was not very convincing. After years of study and a Ph.D. in economics, the answer I gave when my Harvard students asked the same question was not much better.

Nor did that training equip me to provide Dr. Martin Luther King, Jr. answers to a series of questions concerning the economics of inequality, poverty, and racial discrimination that he asked a group of young economists as he was preparing for the Poor People's March in 1968 just prior to his death. The most difficult questions about economics I have ever been asked did not come on my Ph.D. exam or from the characteristically energetic challenges by seminar participants at the University of Chicago. They came, instead, from trade union members in the US clothing industry attending a crash course in economics who wanted to understand the economic impact of the North American Free Trade Agreement, and were not satisfied when I responded with some blackboard economics that, on reflection, I too realized was wrong. When President Nelson Mandela asked me and the other members of a commission he had appointed to design policies and institutions to, as he put it, "erase the footprints of apartheid" in South Africa's labor markets, I mumbled to myself "a tall order" and set to work on the hardest economics problem I had yet encountered.

The result, in the pages that follow, are not blackboard ideas waiting to descend from the ivory tower when suitably polished. It was the other way around. The econometrics papers I wrote on inequality in US education were stimulated by unanswered questions in the background memo I wrote at the request of Senator Robert Kennedy when he was running for president. When a coalition of trade unions and progressive groups asked David Gordon, Thomas Weisskopf, and me to write a memo explaining the faltering performance of the US economy in the 1970s and to suggest strategies that might mitigate its impact on workers and the less well-off, we eventually devoted years to what became a series of replies. The academic papers resulting from this collaboration that eventually appeared in the *American Economic Review* and the *Brookings Papers on Economic Activity* were merely by-products of the exercise, not its purpose.

Truth in advertising requires me to reveal that I lack the people skills necessary to influence public policy, which is why my day job has always been at the blackboard and the keyboard. When I warned Senator Kennedy not to promise the voters that his educational programs would dramatically reduce inequality unless they were coupled with an assault on wealth inequality and racism, another member of his "economics brain trust" chided me (to general nodding by the other brain trusters), "Sam, everyone else in this room is trying to build America up! You're tearing it down!" When I proposed employment subsidies and other market-based jobs policies to combat the rampant joblessness in South Africa's economy, a leading trade unionist publically branded me an "enemy of the working class." The diagnosis of the ills of the US economy that Gordon, Weisskopf, and I offered – that a productivity slowdown and profit squeeze occurred because the booming late 1960s and early 1970s had erased the fear of getting fired, and that labor discipline suffered as a result – gave us the moniker "blame-the-workers economists."

Hoping not to collect any new epithets, but in any case undeterred, in this book I explore policies to implement a more egalitarian distribution of wealth and power without compromising economic efficiency. In the next chapter I provide an overview of an economic strategy based on recent evidence and models showing that the level of economic inequality in the US and many other countries today is not grease for the wheels of economic progress, but sand in the gears. My joint work with Arjun Jayadev presented in the chapter provides a striking example. We show that highly unequal economies (and cities) devote a very substantial fraction of their productive potential to what we call *guard labor* charged, roughly, with keeping the lid on rather than producing goods and services.

Because its objective is to raise productivity (output properly measured per hour of work) rather than total output and because its primary means are a redistribution of wealth and power rather than a redistribution of income, I call this strategy *productivity-enhancing asset redistribution.*

Living standards are ideally measured by what people can do rather than what they have (Sen 1999), and this depends not only on the appropriately measured goods and services available to them (including environmental amenities), but also on the amount of their free time, and other intangibles. Increased productivity permits greater access to either goods and services or free time, or both, making productivity enhancement rather than output growth a more attractive objective.

In Chapter 2 I draw on new developments in the theory of incomplete credit contracts to give an example of how such a strategy might work.

In the next two chapters I address the impact of the increased international mobility of goods and capital on the feasibility and effectiveness of policies designed to insure greater economic security and equality of opportunity. Chapter 3 shows that, while globalization alters the environment in which egalitarian policies work, it makes productivity-enhancing asset-based redistribution a highly effective strategy. The primary obstacle to such policies is political, not economic. Chapter 4, which draws on work with Ugo Pagano, addresses the impact of globalization on the new politics of the welfare state.

In Chapter 5, I use research jointly conducted with Christina Fong and Herbert Gintis to explore the implications of the behavioral economics revolution for understanding the political economy of redistribution. The fact that many people, perhaps most people, are committed to fairness even if it will cost them something suggests a new politics that recognizes the ethical roots of support for redistribution as well as ethical (if sometimes uninformed) reasons for opposition.

I am grateful to my collaborators Christina Fong, Herbert Gintis, Arjun Jayadev, and Ugo Pagano. My former doctoral students Anders Fremstad, Alyssa Schneebaum, and Simon Halliday greatly improved the text. I would also like to thank the Behavioral Sciences Program of the Santa Fe Institute, the University of Siena, and the Russell Sage Foundation for support of this research. I am indebted to the kind staff and the tranquil surroundings of the Certosa di Pontignano for an optimal environment for reflection, research, and writing. The MacArthur Foundation's Research Network on the Costs of Inequality allowed a decade of sustained reflection on the topics raised here; I am grateful to Pranab Bardhan with whom I directed the network and to its members, and to the Foundation for making our collaboration possible. I developed many of the ideas here as a teacher in economics crash courses under the auspices of the Center for Popular Economics (Amherst, Ma.), the International Woodcutters of America (Vancouver, British Columbia), the New Democratic Party of British Columbia and the National Union of Miners (South Africa). I am grateful to all of these organizations and the participants in their programs. Robert Rowthorn's comments on the entire text resulted in numerous improvements. A final thank-you goes to Maurizio Franzini, MarioTiberi, and the other organizers of the Federico Caffè Lecture in Rome, which I delivered in 2007, the response to which stimulated my writing this book.

I dedicate this work to my departed friends Gerald Cohen, who provided solid philosophical foundations for modern egalitarianism, and David Gordon, who laid out the economics of a just and democratic society. More than outstanding scholars, they were also engaged in changing the world, as the titles of their last (posthumous) books attest: *Why Not Socialism?* and *Fat and Mean: The Corporate Squeeze of Working Americans and the Myth of Managerial Downsizing.*

Santa Fe, New Mexico

1

The new economics of inequality and redistribution

Socialism, radical democracy, social democracy, and other egalitarian movements have flourished where they successfully crafted the demands of distributive justice into an economic strategy capable of addressing the problem of scarcity, and thereby promised to improve living standards on the average. Redistributing land to the tiller, social insurance, egalitarian wage policies, central planning, and providing adequate health care and schooling for all have been attractive when they promised to link a more just distribution of economic reward to enhanced performance of the economic system as a whole.

For this reason economic analysis has always been central to the construction of more democratic and egalitarian alternatives to capitalism, as well as to reforms of capitalism itself. Keynesian economics, for example, supported state regulation of the macro economy and also provided a rationale for income redistribution to the less well-off who, by spending a larger portion of their incomes, could be relied upon to generate higher and more reliable levels of demand for consumer goods, and thereby to sustain greater macroeconomic stability and higher levels of employment. Similarly, the model of general competitive exchange was deployed by socialists from Oskar Lange and Enrico Barone in the 1930s to Pranab Bardhan and John Roemer two generations later to demonstrate the possibility and advantages of democratic planning.

But today it appears that the left has run out of economic models. Keynesian policies to modulate fluctuations in aggregate demand are essential, but do not provide a foundation for a long-term egalitarian strategy. And while looming environmental catastrophe has underlined the need for public interventions to override the private-profit motive, centralized economic planning is incapable of regulating a complex, knowledge-based economy.

This is not to say that the left has abandoned the construction of alternatives to capitalism, as a reading of Bardhan and Roemer (1992), van Parijs (1995), Roemer (1996), Cohen (2009), and Wright (2010) will indicate. Nor have economists shrunk from the challenge of understanding the new global capitalist order (Glyn 2006, Bourguignon 2012) and designing policies to alleviate poverty (van Parijs and van der Veen 1986, Banerjee and Duflo 2011).

Yet even among egalitarians the conviction is widespread that while some combination of social democracy, market socialism, and workplace democracy would be preferable on democratic or egalitarian grounds to the capitalism we know, only capitalism has a workable answer to the problem of scarcity. Economic theory has proven, one hears, that any but cosmetic modifications of capitalism in the direction of equality and democratic control will exact a heavy toll of reduced economic performance.

Yet economic theory suggests no such thing. On the contrary, there are compelling economic arguments and ample empirical support for the proposition that there exist changes in the rules of the economic game which can foster both greater economic equality and improved economic performance. To see how this could be done, I need to explain how wealth inequality may be an impediment to productivity.

Inequality, institutions, and economic performance

First, some terms. *Co-ordination failures* occur when the independent actions of agents lead to outcomes less desirable for some, and not better for anyone than could have been achieved in the presence of co-ordinated action. Economists term such an outcome *Pareto-inefficient*, meaning that there exists some technically feasible change in the current state such that some would be better off and none worse off. A *Pareto improvement* is a change that has this property; a *Pareto-optimal* state is one from which no Pareto improvements are possible. The latter is really a misnomer, because states with this benign designation may be highly unjust. (The terms are due to the Italian economist Vilfredo Pareto, 1848–1923.)

Examples of co-ordination failures are environmental pollution, unemployment, traffic jams, the creation of super-bugs through the misuse of antibiotics, spam, and the commonly observed inability of employers and workers to implement mutually beneficial changes in work rules and technology. The latter case – concerning employers and workers – is termed a *principal–agent problem*, the principal being the employer who pays a wage in return for the work time of the agent. Another important principal–agent interaction occurs in credit markets, where wealthy lenders (principals) lend money to borrowers (agents) in return for a promise of repayment with interest. Unlike traffic jams, in which all cars are (more or less) equal, principals and agents engage in asymmetric interactions: They differ in the actions each can take. The employer can offer a higher or lower wage, the worker can work hard or sleep on the job; the banker can charge a high or low interest rate, the borrower can repay or default.

These and other principal–agent relationships result in Pareto-inefficient outcomes. Compared to the situation in which both the employer and worker are taking the actions that maximize their objectives given the actions taken by the other (the *Nash equilibrium*), there exists a combination of a higher wage and greater work effort under which both the employer and the worker would be better off. And at the Nash equilibrium some would-be workers – even if identical to those employed – will be without a job. Similarly (as we will see in the next chapter), some would-be borrowers will be excluded from the credit market entirely, even when the projects they would implement are superior to those being funded. Where credit transactions do occur, there exists a Pareto improvement over the Nash equilibrium: one in which the lender charges a lower rate of interest and the borrower takes fewer risks with his money.

Pareto-inefficient outcomes occur in other principal–agent relationships too, for example those between landlords and tenants (either agrarian or residential). Most relationships among people of different classes (in the traditional Marxian sense) are principal–agent relationships. Traffic jams and the threat of super-bugs are not.

But co-ordination failures indicated by these examples of Pareto-inefficient outcomes occur in principal–agent relationships for the same reason that traffic jams happen and super-bugs proliferate. Co-ordination failures arise because some of the effects of an individual's actions on others – a more crowded highway, second-hand smoke, or a job well done, or the prudent use of borrowed funds so that repayment is assured – cannot be specified in an enforceable contract. The motorist who decides to drive downtown during rush hour cannot be charged for the additional congestion that she creates. The borrower's promise to repay will not mean much if he has gambled and lost it all. The source of the co-ordination failure in each case is not the absence of competition, or rigid wages, or "sticky prices," or "short-term maximizing," or any of the usual culprits. The problem is that the relevant contracts are incomplete. These and related cases are studied in detail in my microeconomics textbook (Bowles 2004). I use the broader term "co-ordination failures" (rather than the common "market failures") because, as these examples indicate, many of the failures take place in arenas other than markets.

The extent of co-ordination failures depends on what may be termed the *structure of economic governance*: the rules of ownership, forms of competition, and norms and conventions that regulate the incentives and constraints faced by economic actors, and hence that determine the nature of co-ordination failures and their feasible solutions. The wealth of nations, as Adam Smith knew, depends critically on the structure of economic governance (or economic institutions for short); and the same can be said for the wealth of communities and firms (Acemoglu, Johnson, and Robinson 2005 and Acemoglu and Robinson, 2012). Ideally, a structure of governance is a means of avoiding or attenuating co-ordination failures, but there is nothing in the process determining the evolution of governance structures that insures this result. Governance structures may endure because they are favored by powerful groups for whom they secure a large slice of a given pie, not because these structures foster the growth of the pie itself.

The relationship between inequality and how productively a society uses its resources is thus mediated by the structure of economic governance. Governance structures also critically influence the degree of inequality. Correspondingly, the feasibility of distinct forms of governance is itself strongly influenced by the degree of inequality and, in particular, by the nature and distribution of property rights. For example, a co-operative-based governance structure in which those who supply labor to the production process also own the tools and equipment with which they work is hardly feasible where workers are very poor. A summary of the causal relationships between structures of governance, wealth inequality, and economic performance appears in Figure 1.1.

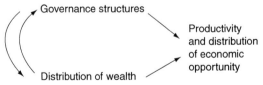

Figure 1.1 *Governance structure, wealth inequality, productivity, and inequality of opportunity*

I will define a change in governance structures as *productivity-enhancing* if the winners could compensate the losers (which would make the change a Pareto improvement), except that the implied compensation need not be carried out or even be implementable under the informational conditions and other incentive problems in the economy. The proposals developed in this book are motivated by the first key idea: *Inequality is an impediment to economic performance when it precludes implementation of productivity-enhancing governance structures.* There are three reasons why this is the case.

The first concerns the inefficient incentive structures that arise in economies with highly unequal asset distributions. An example may make this clear. Consider a single owner of a machine who hires a single worker to operate the machine who has no wealth. The worker has little reason to supply a high level of effort, since the worker is paid a given wage and the owner is the residual claimant on the income associated with the asset and hence receives the profit from the worker's labor. The *residual claimant* owns whatever remains (the residual) after all fixed claims (in this case the wage paid by the owner) are settled. Thus, without costly monitoring, productivity in the firm will suffer. But monitoring uses up resources that could have otherwise been productively employed. A rental contract in which the worker rents the machine from the owner for a fixed sum and becomes residual claimant on the entire income stream of the firm would of course avoid this particular incentive problem. But this solution to the effort–incentive difficulty simply displaces the conflict of interest to the issue of the treatment of the machine – in this case, the firm's capital stock itself. For the worker would then be residual claimant on the income produced by the machine, but not on the value of the machine itself, and hence would have little incentive to maintain the asset. Since the worker has no wealth, he or she cannot be the owner of the machine.

The generic problem here is that behaviors critical to high levels of productivity – hard work, maintenance of productive equipment, risk-taking, the production and use of knowledge and the like – are difficult to monitor and hence cannot be fully specified in any contract enforceable at low cost. As a result, key economic actors, workers and managers, for example, cannot capture the productivity effects of their actions as they would if, for instance, they were the residual claimants on the resulting income stream and asset value.

The result of these incentive problems is that a highly concentrated ownership of capital goods is often inefficient. We will see (Chapter 2) that there may exist a more egalitarian distribution, in which the worker becomes the owner of the firm's capital goods which, by more effectively addressing the incentive, monitoring, and maintenance problems involved, allows general improvements in well-being (including possible compensation for the former owner).

This being the case, one might wonder why the redistribution does not come about spontaneously. If worker ownership of the firm avoids incentive problems and supervision costs, it might be thought that owning the firm will be worth more to the worker than to the employer. But if this is the case, the worker would profit by borrowing to purchase the firm's capital stock. However, an asset-poor worker cannot borrow large sums (we will see why in the next chapter), and so he or she cannot purchase the firm's capital stock. Furthermore, the worker would be unlikely to agree to assume the risk of concentrated ownership of a risky asset, even if it could be financed. For this reason inefficient distributions of property rights – in this case the firm not being owned by the worker – may prove immune to disruption through private contracting despite the existence of other, more efficient distributions. More technically, inefficient property-right distributions may be sustained as a Nash equilibrium in a competitive equilibrium.

This one-worker firm example makes an important point, but it is unreal. Modern economies cannot avoid such incentive problems by implementing the simple property-ownership structures appropriate to an idealized Robinson Crusoe world of individual production. The economies of scale that characterize all contemporary economies make team production ubiquitous. In a capitalist firm the workers will shirk on the employer; in a co-op they will free ride on each other. These and related incentive problems will arise under any conceivable set of property distributions and institutional arrangements. So letting "the worker" own the machine is no magic bullet: co-ordination failures among a team of workers and (as we will see in the next chapter) their possibly over-prudent approach to risk-taking would have to be addressed. Nonetheless, differing levels of wealth inequality permit structures of economic governance that differ markedly in the costliness of the incentive problems to which they give rise, highly skewed wealth distributions supporting particularly inefficiency-prone governance structures.

A second reason why greater equality may enhance productivity arises because, where contracts are incomplete, the resulting co-ordination problems may be attenuated if people are intrinsically motivated to do a good job, to tell the truth, and to care about and to trust one another; and these sentiments are often difficult to sustain between the haves and the have-nots. Kenneth Arrow (1971:22) writes:

> It is useful for individuals to have some trust in each other's word. In the absence of trust it would be very costly to arrange for alternative sanctions and guarantees, and many opportunities for mutually beneficial cooperation would have to be forgone ... norms of social behavior, including ethical and moral codes [may be] ... reactions of society to compensate for market failures.

In addition to the invisible hand of competition and the fist of command, a well-governed society must also rely on the handshake of trust.

One of the possible productivity effects of greater equality may thus operate through the political and cultural consequences of redistribution. A well-run welfare state or a relatively equal distribution of property holdings may foster the social solidarity necessary to support co-operation and trust. These and related sentiments frequently provide the basis for low-cost solutions to co-ordination failures.

A third way in which equality may enhance productivity arises because institutional structures supporting high levels of inequality are often costly to maintain. Solving economic problems requires a state empowered to intervene effectively in the economy. But an activist state is capable of using its power not only to improve economic efficiency, but also to redistribute income in response to populist pressures. For this reason economic elites may prefer an ineffective state in an inefficient economy to a strong state in an efficient economy. Moreover, states in highly unequal societies are often obliged to commit a large fraction of the economy's productive potential simply to enforcing the rules of the game from which the inequalities flow: soldiers, police officers, prison wardens, and others in the ranks of what Arjun Jayadev and I call *guard labor* constituting large fractions of the labor force (Jayadev and Bowles 2005, Bowles and Jayadev 2007).

The private sector also incurs costs in enforcing inequality, in such forms as high levels of expenditure on work supervision and security personnel. Indeed, one might count high levels of unemployment itself as one of the enforcement costs of inequality, because the threat of job loss contributes to employers' labor discipline strategies. In less conflictual conditions, unemployed labor might be allocated to productive activities (we provide an illustration of how this might be done in Chapter 3). Moreover, in highly inegalitarian societies the insecurity of property rights is often widespread, militating against long-term investments by the rich and the poor alike.

Curious about the extent of and reasons for guard labor, Jayadev and I wondered if the demand for private guards was particularly high in US cities with very unequal distributions of income. Figure 1.2 shows what we found.

We also adopted a much broader concept of guard labor and sought to determine the amount of time devoted to the enforcement of claims on resources, including the protection of property rights and efforts to secure distributional advantage where contracts are absent or incomplete. We included supervisory labor, private guards, police, judicial and prison employees, military and civilian employees of the department of defense (and those producing military equipment), the unemployed, and prisoners. The data for the US are in Figure 1.3, and a cross-country comparison of the guard labor burden is in Figure 1.4. As in the case of private security guards in US cities, the extent of guard labor is correlated with measures of economic polarization (and also simply inequality of income), and varies inversely with measures of social welfare spending, as shown in Figures 1.5a–1.5b.

Where economic interactions are long on conflict and short on trust, technologies may also be chosen with the objective of improving an employer's bargaining power vis-à-vis his employees, reducing monitoring costs, or otherwise improving the labor discipline environment. Here is an example. When US trucking companies installed on-board computers during the 1980s, they vastly improved their ability to monitor the actions of the drivers (Baker and Hubbard 2000). Trip recorders provided the company with verifiable information on the speed, idle time, and other details of the operation of the truck about which there was a conflict of interest between the driver and the company. For example, the cost of operating the trucks (paid by the company) increased with the speed of the truck.

Drivers preferred to drive faster than the cost-minimizing speed, and to take longer breaks. Drivers who owned their trucks were residual claimants on their revenues minus these

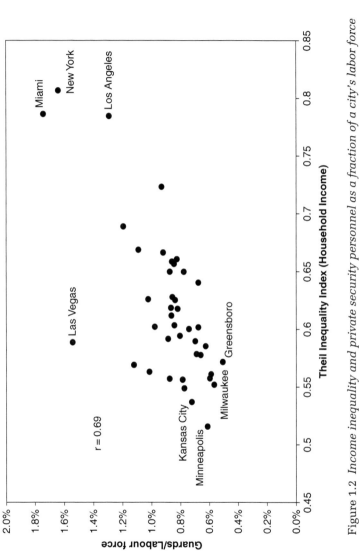

Figure 1.2 *Income inequality and private security personnel as a fraction of a city's labor force*

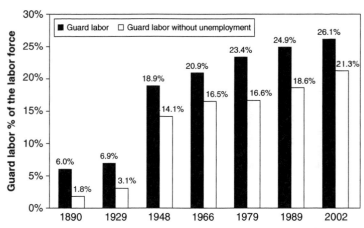

Figure 1.3 *The emergence of a garrison economy: guard labor in the US.*
The unemployment measure is the excess of observed unemployment over an estimate of unavoidable "frictional" unemployment. Source: Bowles and Jayadev, (2007).

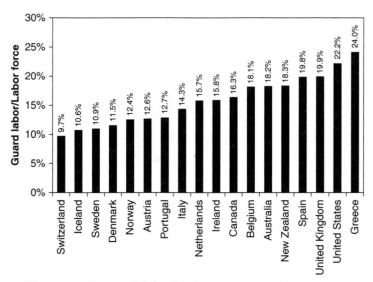

Figure 1.4 *The guard-labor burden across countries.*
Police and private security guards are not included due to lack of comparable data. Source: Bowles and Jayadev, (2007).

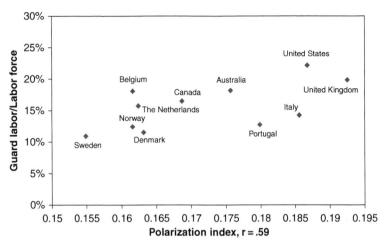

Figure 1.5a *Economic polarization and guard labor as a fraction of a nation's labor force.* Source: Bowles and Jayadev, (2007).

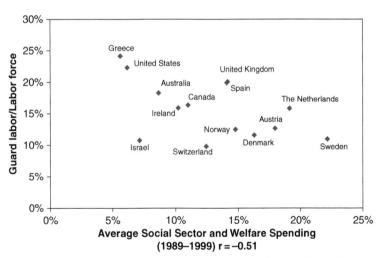

Figure 1.5b *Teachers vs. guards? Social spending and guard labor.* Source: Bowles and Jayadev, (2007).

and other costs, and hence, of course, internalized the costs of fuel and depreciation, realizing significant savings as a result. For this reason, prior to the introduction of trip recorders, owner-operators successfully competed with company fleets on those runs for which the conflicts of interest between drivers and companies were particularly strong.

Using the trip recorders, companies were able to write contracts based on the speed at which the truck was driven, and to provide drivers other incentives to act in the companies' interests. Unlike other on-board computers (the electronic vehicle managements systems, or EVMSs), the trip recorders provided no improvement in co-ordination between truckers and dispatchers, as the information was available to the company only on the completion of the trip. The sole function of the trip recorders was to improve the contractibility of aspects of drivers' behaviors in which there was a conflicting interest between the drivers and the companies. By improving the company's contractual opportunities, the trip recorders had two effects. First, drivers in trucks with recorders drove slower, boosting company profit; and second, the market share of owner-operators declined.

Another example of the choice of technology makes clear that the exercise of power is sometimes an explicit motive in the innovation process. A major production bottleneck in the late nineteenth-century California food-canning industry was the highly skilled work of putting tops on the cans, or "capping" as it was called (Phillips and Brown 1986). The small number of difficult-to-replace cappers exacted substantial rents from their employers because of their indispensable role in production and the perishable nature of the goods at harvest time. The invention of a contraption called Cox's capper changed this; but the firms that avidly purchased the device did not initially use it to cap cans, as it was not cost-effective at the going wages. Rather, it was deployed as a part of the firm's rent-seeking strategy and simply held in abeyance should the (human) cappers' demands become excessive. Writing twenty-six years after he invented the contraption, James Cox recalled the canning owners' strategic need for the mechanical capper: "the helplessness of the canner [vis-à-vis the human cappers] made him a willing advocate of every mechanical means, and made possible the working out, through frequent failures and heavy losses, the perfected mechanical means now in use."

These three reasons why inequality may be bad for productivity – by diluting incentives, discouraging trust, and diverting resources from productive uses to enforcing the rules of the game or driving a harder bargain – suggest that the nature and distribution of property rights critically affect the performance of the economy. This view reflects what may be termed the new economics of property, in which property is not simply a claim on the residual income deriving from an asset, but also the right to control access to the asset and disposition over its use. This view motivates a second key idea: *where hard work, innovation, maintenance of an asset, and other behaviors essential to productivity cannot be specified in costlessly enforceable contracts, some distributions of property rights are more efficient than others; in particular there exists a class of distributions that are both more egalitarian and more efficient than the concentrated asset-holding observed in most capitalist economies.*

Market failures and state failures

It should be clear from the above that devising governance structures capable of supporting both greater equality and higher living standards requires a fundamental rethinking of relationships between markets, states, and communities. The necessary reconstruction of political economy must therefore confront three widespread prejudices common among social scientists and political actors alike.

The first is that competitive markets determine prices that measure at least approximately the real scarcity of goods and for this reason allocate resources efficiently. For the most part they do not; as we will see, the considerable contribution of markets to effective economic governance lies elsewhere.

The second prejudice, particularly widespread among egalitarians, is that in a suitably democratic society, government intervention can efficiently supplant the private provision of goods and services where market failures occur. But state failures in the production and delivery of goods and services are as ubiquitous as market failures. As in the case of markets, the distinctive capacities of the state in the process of economic governance are frequently overlooked by the advocates of interventionist policies.

The third prejudice, common across much of the political spectrum, is to see communities as anachronistic rather than modern institutions and to suppose that whatever social value communities have, their contribution to contemporary economic governance is minimal. By a *community* I mean a group of individuals whose interactions are long-term, frequent, and personal. Families, residential neighborhoods, and workplaces are communities in this sense. Moreover, while community governance structures cannot be subsumed under the rubrics of state and market, their viability critically depends on the structure of states and markets, and in particular on the nature and distribution of property rights implied by the structure of states and markets.

In sum, the prejudices of conservative policy stem from its recognition of weaknesses in the state, but not in the market as governance structures. This selective treatment leads to the view that the state is an arena of wasteful rent-seeking and inefficient distortions of competitive prices, while the market economy is efficient, a view from which exclusive reliance upon the market ineluctably follows. Advocates of egalitarian economic policy, by contrast, while treating the market system as riddled with failures, have often failed to recognize the limitations of the state as a governance structure, and hence have treated the state as an effective instrument for

Economy / State	No market failures	Market failures
No state failures	Both *laissez-faire* and planning can support optimal allocations	Keynesian and other state interventions can support optimal allocations
State failures	*Laissez-faire* with minimal state can support optimal allocations	Market/state/community complementarity can support second-best allocations

Figure 1.6 *Alternative approaches to economic policy*

the implementation of economic objectives. Both strands of political economy have overlooked the critical role of communities as governance structures.

These alternatives are summarized in Figure 1.6. The optimism of post-Second World War Keynesian policies, and that of the neo-liberal policies that supplanted them, can be seen to flow from the choice of assumption concerning the location of co-ordination failures (the lower-left to upper-right diagonal in Figure 1.6). My approach recognizes co-ordination failures in both the state and market, and achieves only those (generally *second-best*) allocations compatible with feasible incentive structures. (A *second-best* allocation is not *Pareto-efficient*, but Pareto improvements, while technically feasible, cannot be implemented given the existing contracts and other institutions.)

Figure 1.6 also includes a fourth policy approach (the upper-left corner) that does not recognize co-ordination problems in either economy or state. This obviously utopian position implies that in the absence of market failures such as externalities, increasing returns to scale, and cyclical volatility, both *laissez-faire* and central planning can support first-best (that is, Pareto-efficient) allocations.

The egalitarian asset-based redistribution idea is an alternative to the more common egalitarian strategy that accepts the given distribution of wealth and seeks to override market outcomes through tax and transfer policies designed to attenuate the consequences of concentrated ownership. But if the current degree of asset inequality is taken as given, market-determined rewards will be correspondingly unequal, so the egalitarian project becomes one of superseding market outcomes and thereby undermining the beneficial disciplining effects of market competition.

A more promising approach is to find a way in which markets will implement more egalitarian outcomes. This can be done by first identifying those aspects of the concentrated ownership of assets that give rise to perverse incentives and costly enforcement strategies and then to devise asset redistributions that can attenuate the resulting co-ordination failures without introducing their own costly incentive problems. In contrast to income-based egalitarian strategies, which are rarely better than productivity-neutral (and often a lot worse), asset-based egalitarianism can in principle be productivity-enhancing. This is true both because it can implement more efficient distributions of residual claimancy and control rights and because redistributing assets addresses a major cause of unequal incomes, and thus gives greater scope for markets to do what they are good at: identifying losers – firms that fail to produce good products at competitive prices – and getting them out of the game.

Markets, of course, also discipline the egalitarian policy-maker, who must design interventions that will result in a distribution of property rights that is sustainable not only politically but also economically. Political sustainability is always difficult, for the well-to-do will always deploy their resources to reverse egalitarian wealth redistribution.

But economic sustainability is no less daunting a challenge. Here is a cautionary tale. The redistribution of land to small-holders in Chile during the early 1970s was intended to benefit the poor, in part by placing residual claimancy in the hands of the farmer, and thereby providing incentives for both greater investment and greater labor effort, leading to higher levels of productivity (Jarvis 1989, Carter, Barham, and Mesbah 1996). The land transfers coincided with a boom in the market for exported fruit. But few of the land-reform beneficiaries had the capital to finance the long gestation period for tree crops, and credit was generally not available to small-holders. Moreover, the volatility of fruit prices would have exposed the farmers to risks which they could not buffer by means of borrowing. As a result, few of the poor farmers shifted to fruit production. At the same time, the value of their land rose dramatically as a result of the fruit boom. Unable to take advantage of the favorable price of fruit, by the early 1990s 57 percent of the original 48,000 beneficiaries had sold their land. The transfer of wealth to the poor had been accomplished, but the realignment of incentives intended by the land reform had failed, because the farmers were still too poor to borrow the funds that would have allowed them to take advantage of the land and to buffer themselves from the risks. The moral of the story is that the increase in the farmers' wealth was insufficient to overcome their risk aversion and exclusion from credit markets, so the "land to the tiller" rationale of the program failed.

This example demonstrates a third key idea: *It is pointless to introduce policies that subsequently will be undone by the private transactions of its beneficiaries or others; a policy is implementable if its intended results can be sustained when all of those affected take whatever actions they prefer under the new conditions* (technically, the intended outcome is a Nash equilibrium). We will address the problem of implementability of egalitarian policies in the next two chapters.

Is equality passé?

My confidence that such implementable productivity-enhancing asset redistributions can be affected may seem out of step with the pervasive contemporary scepticism concerning the viability of egalitarian alternatives. But the intellectual foundations of *equality pessimism*, as I have termed this frame of mind, have been badly shaken. Recent research has both questioned the presumption that economic performance is best promoted by *laissez-faire* policies and cast doubt upon the existence of the *efficiency–equity trade-off*, which asserts that the pursuit of egalitarian objectives necessarily impairs productivity and thus imposes a cost on living standards on average. This fabled trade-off is a staple of blackboard economics, making an appearance in most introductory texts. (An influential statement is Okun 1975.)

Until the early 1990s nobody had really bothered to look for it in the real world. When they did, the trade-off turned out to be more like a unicorn than hard science. A comparison of the economic performance among nations revealed no such trade-off. Countries experiencing rapid productivity growth between the 1960s and the 1980s, including China, Singapore, Taiwan and South Korea, exhibited a degree of economic equality and a level of state involvement in economic decision-making considerably greater than in the relatively *laissez-faire* industrialized countries which, in the same period, experienced weak productivity growth and increases in economic inequality. The contrast with the relatively stagnant and highly unequal Latin American economies was even starker. Several studies supported these findings: My co-authors and I (Bowles, Gordon, and Weisskopf 1990) found that across ten advanced capitalist economies, the more unequal the distribution of income, the lower was both the long-term rate of growth of output per employed person and the investment share of output (a conventional measure of economic good health). Persson and Tabellini (1996) showed that inequality and growth in gross domestic product were negatively correlated in a cross-section of sixty-seven nations, as well as in long time series for nine advanced capitalist nations. Alesina and Rodrik (1994) found that a measure of asset (land) inequality was inversely associated with economic growth in a sample of thirty-nine countries.

However, cross-national comparisons of inequality and macroeconomic performance are of limited use in assessing the effects of policies to reduce inequality on economic performance. A policy-maker or a citizen is interested not in the *correlates of equality* but in the *effects of egalitarian policies*. The fact that more equal countries have more rapid rates of economic growth could well be accounted for by a statistical association between measures of equality and unmeasured causes of economic growth. Perhaps the correlation of equality and rapid productivity increase arises because Koreans are both exceptionally hardworking and fair-minded while the British are indolent and tolerant of inequality. Determining the effects of a decision to redistribute land or to raise the minimum wage requires the study of the evolution of policies and their outcomes over time.

Thus, a better indicator of a positive relationship between egalitarian institutions and policies on the one hand and economic performance on the other is the fact that the thirteen largest advanced capitalist countries, taken as a whole, grew faster under the aegis of the post-Second World War welfare state than in any other period for which the relevant data exist. In historical retrospect, the epoch of the ascendant welfare state and social democracy was capitalism's golden age. This relationship is exhibited in Figure 1.7. Though others have used these data to make the case, I do not conclude that greater equality *per se* promotes high levels of economic performance. But a more modest inference seems inescapable: Under favorable institutional circumstances, policies to promote greater equality are not incompatible with the rapid growth of productivity and other valued macroeconomic outcomes.

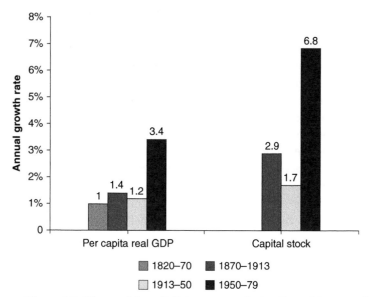

Figure 1.7 *The world capitalist economy during the golden age of trade unions and the welfare state: 1950–79.*
Source: Glyn, Hughes, Lipietz, and Singh (1990).

"Equality pessimism" thus finds little support in the empirical record of macroeconomic performance. Rather, the sense that egalitarian projects may now be unfeasible appears to derive more from the demise of a particular model of redistribution and from the way in which global competition is said to constrain the autonomy of nation states in their pursuit of egalitarian objectives. The optimism of the golden age of egalitarian economic policy – roughly the first three decades following the Second World War – was fostered by the Keynesian belief that the expansion of publicly funded social services and transfers, as well as wage increases in the private sector, would promote full employment, macroeconomic stability, and productivity growth. This belief served to minimize political opposition to egalitarian redistribution by promising "soft redistribution": even the wealthy would benefit from policies to stabilize and expand aggregate demand and provide adequate schooling and medical care for the workforce.

Underlying this faith – at least in the English-speaking countries – was a macroeconomic model that could be termed "national Keynesianism." The first of its three main tenets was that the level of output in a national economy is limited by the level of aggregate demand for goods and services. The second tenet equated aggregate demand to the home market. The third held that more egalitarian distributions of income support higher levels of aggregate demand. Egalitarian redistribution was thus doubly blessed: It promised "soft redistribution," addressing the needs of the less well-off, while promoting the general interest of abundance for all.

The evidence does not support the third, and most critical, of these tenets, however, and the second tenet, upon which the third is based, is also flawed. An econometric study I conducted with the French economist Robert Boyer (Bowles and Boyer 1995) of the US, France, the UK, Japan, and Germany over the post-war period shows that increased wages are unlikely to lead to an increase in aggregate demand, and that this is particularly the case the more open the economy is to exports and imports. Also, even in the cases where Boyer and I found that increasing the real wage would expand aggregate demand, the estimated effect is small, and is insufficient to support a positive relationship between the real wage and the rate of investment. Thus, even if a general wage increase were to expand a nation's employment in the short run, it seems likely that it would diminish private investment, thus jeopardizing the long-run viability of this particular egalitarian strategy (at least if implemented singly). The estimated effects of increased unemployment benefits and other income redistributive measures on aggregate demand and investment are no more promising.

Smaller and more internationally open economies are unlikely to be exceptions to these findings. Thus, there is some doubt concerning the relevance, even in the heyday of social democracy, of a Keynesian wage-led growth regime. The positive macroeconomic effects of social-democratic policies in Nordic Europe, for example, are more plausibly attributed to such productivity-enhancing policies as unifying wage structures across industries (which drove inefficient firms out of business) and investment in education and health than to the aggregate demand effects of wage increases. Moene and Wallerstein (1995b) make this argument quite compellingly. The first tenet is not wrong: Demand constraints continue to limit output and employment. But the global integration of national economies has rendered the level of output in each country increasingly sensitive to worldwide demand conditions and to the competitive position of each economy, and less dependent on the consumption goods demanded by a nation's wage earners. Some of the most successful social-democratic economies were already highly integrated in the global marketplace prior to the introduction of their particular brand of egalitarian policies.

As a result, attention has shifted from the demand-enhancing effect of high wages and social expenditures to the effect of wages and other redistributive policies on costs and productivity. With the analytical underpinnings of soft redistribution thus shaken and the political viability of hard redistribution doubted, the egalitarian project has stalled. The reorientation of economic policy to supply-side rather than demand-side problems appears to have entailed a corresponding shift from egalitarian redistribution to its converse: policies promoting greater inequality, justified by the promise of long-run, trickle-down effects.

The new emphasis on long-term productivity growth is entirely welcome; and arguments for greater emphasis on other supply-side issues are compelling. But the abandonment of the egalitarian project is a *non sequitur*. Rather than a simple correspondence between demand-side economics and egalitarian policy on the one hand and supply-side

Distributional aspect of policy

		Egalitarian	Trickle-down
Diagnosis of the problem	Demand side	Left Keynesianism	Low wage export-led growth "Military Keynesianism"
	Supply side	Productivity-enhancing redistributions	"Washington consensus" IMF structural adjustment policy

Figure 1.8 *An expanded policy menu: diagnosis and distribution*

economics and trickle-down policy on the other, there is a complex array of choices. For example, the Keynesian focus on demand need not favor egalitarian policies. As we have observed, in a world of globally integrated national economies, aggregate demand may be fostered by a redistribution from wages to profits, rather than by the reverse. The effect of upwards redistribution of income on investment and net exports could well offset the decline in workers' demand for consumer goods. And even more surprisingly, the focus on supply-side problems does not entail trickle-down policies: Egalitarian redistributive policies can be productivity-enhancing. The expanded menu of choices is presented in Figure 1.8.

A further implication of the globalization of production is that it may be very costly to redistribute against the owners of factors of production that are globally mobile, notably capital. The point is easily exaggerated, often by opponents of redistribution. The process of investment is still primarily national: The vast majority of investment in every major country is of domestic origin. Moreover, most international movements of direct investment are among high-wage countries, not from these countries to the low-wage economies. But any sharp reduction in the after-tax rate of profit expected by wealth holders in any particular country may provoke responses capable of devastating an egalitarian program. The response of investors to the election of the socialists

François Mitterrand in France and Salvador Allende in Chile are examples. The mobility of goods and finance thus does not preclude egalitarian policies, but it does substantially raise the political and economic costs of policies that are purely redistributive, if among the losers are those who are free to move.

Conflict and co-ordination

I stress productivity growth as an objective because the long-run gains in living standards obtainable through redistribution are limited by the size of the pie, while the benefits of productivity growth, including increased leisure, are cumulative. Productivity growth means an increase in output per unit of labor in which the measure of both inputs and outputs takes account of environmental effects. As defined, productivity growth is both conceptually and practically distinct from other criteria such as income growth or "competitiveness." Further, policies designed to reduce working time are consistent with the objective of productivity growth, but not with the objective of output growth. Since the benefits of productivity growth are cumulative, if one considers a sufficiently long-term horizon, redistributions that are productivity-reducing are difficult to support, even if one's sole concern were the well-being of the less well-off: After some years, they would have had a higher living standard under the less egalitarian status quo.

For example, suppose the bottom half of the income distribution receives 25 percent of total income. Equalizing income would on the average double the income of members of the bottom half of the distribution. Continuous productivity growth at a modest rate of 2.5 percent per year for 28 years could also double the income of each member of the bottom half of the distribution, with no change in the degree of inequality. Of course, economic welfare may depend on one's relative, as well as one's absolute, economic position.

To the extent that this is true, sustained productivity growth overestimates welfare growth for the less well-off. However, economic welfare may also depend on one's expected future absolute economic position relative to one's current position, in which case sustained productivity growth underestimates welfare growth for all persons.

A single-minded desire to redivide the pie has diverted some egalitarians from the task of producing a better pie. More precisely, the characteristic leftist focus on the conflictual aspect of social interactions has obscured its co-ordination aspect. Interactions typically exhibit both aspects, but we can define polar cases. A *pure conflict interaction* between two people is one in which all possible outcomes can be ranked as better for one and worse for the other. (All of the outcomes are Pareto-efficient.) Zero-sum games are an example. Conversely, *a pure co-ordination interaction* is one in which all feasible outcomes can be ranked such that if one outcome is better than another for one of the actors, the same will be true for the other actor. (There is only one Pareto-efficient outcome and, given any two distinct feasible outcomes, one is preferred by both ["*Pareto-preferred*"] to the other.)

The exploitation of one person by another may be a pure conflict, while a traffic jam may be nearly a pure co-ordination problem. The difference is illustrated in Figure 1.9, which presents a measure of well-being for two individuals (it does not matter what it is – income, "utility," or whatever), with each dot the result of a particular outcome of their interaction. Which outcome occurs depends both on the economic institutions regulating their interaction, and on the actions taken by each. Person I is evidently advantaged, as all of I's outcomes (102, 103, etc.) are far better than any of II's (2, 3, etc.). If the possible outcomes included only points **a** through **e**, it would be a pure conflict game; if only **f** and one of **c** or **d** were possible, it would be a pure co-ordination game. If point **f** obtains under existing institutions, and if **c** and **d** are the other technically feasible outcomes, getting to any of them may be considered to

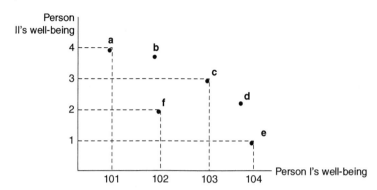

Figure 1.9 *Conflict and co-ordination.*

be more important than struggling over which one to choose: Solving the co-ordination aspect of the problem may be more important than resolving the conflict aspect. Point **f** indicates what we have called a co-ordination failure: At least one point superior to **f** for both people is possible, but is not obtained due to the lack of co-ordinated action of the two.

The logic of productivity-enhancing redistributions is that movements from **f** to **b** are possible, and that movements in a north-easterly direction in the figure ("soft redistribution") may be a more promising strategy than movements to the north-west ("hard redistribution"), even if the claims of justice would support the latter. This example should not be taken literally, of course. There will necessarily be losers in any major change in property rights or other aspects of the institutions that co-ordinate economic activity. The fundamental point is not that all changes should be strictly Pareto-improving (no losers), but that egalitarian redistributions should be productivity-enhancing.

If mutually beneficial solutions to co-ordination failures exist, it may be asked why they are not adopted. Why, that is, are co-ordination failures so common? The answer, I think, is that privileged groups often prefer the economic institutions resulting in **f** to an alternative set of institutions that has all the other points as possible outcomes, due to the fear that, among these, point *a* will be chosen.

A generalization of this example is as follows. The holders of concentrated wealth often find themselves in opposition to changes in the rules of the game necessary to solve co-ordination failures. Even in the shadow of the Great Depression, many American businessmen initially opposed Keynesian aggregate demand management not because they doubted that these policies would boost their profits, but because they feared what other policies a more intervention-ist state might adopt. Co-ordination failures arise because people cannot make binding agreements among themselves. Solving co-ordination failures therefore frequently involves introducing institutions for the enforcement of collective decisions. But the only broadly legitimate way to make these decisions is by majority rule, a process in which the very rich may be out-voted, and institutions created to solve one problem are readily deployed for other ends. Thus, where the wealthy exercise sufficient power, the result may be the failure to adopt a superior institutional structure capa-ble of averting co-ordination problems by facilitating collec-tively binding agreements.

To analyze how governance structures can impede desirable solutions to co-ordination failures, I will use a concrete exam-ple to which Figure 1.9 applies. Person I, let us say, is the owner of a firm, and II is the firm's only worker. The two actors each decide whether to select one of two production inputs: The worker may apply high or low effort to the job, and the owner may or may not devote resources to modernizing the firm's capital stock. Call the two options High and Low for short. Let us assume, realistically I believe, that these decisions are not easy to reverse: The investment, once committed, is costly to redeploy, and the workers' agreement to new work rules or revelation of how hard she can actually work, once conceded, is difficult to withdraw. When they each provide Low, the result is indicated by point **f** in Figure 1.9: The worker gets 2, the owner gets 102. They could do better, but the problem is that each could also do worse. This is the challenge facing the governance structure.

If both select High, the combination of effective labor in a modernized plant yields any of points **b**, **c**, or **d**, depending on how the gains are shared. If the outcome is **c**, for example, the worker gets 3 and the owner gets 103. However, in many situations each will prefer to select Low while the other selects High; the worker would prefer less intense work in a more modern plant (point **a**), while the capitalist would prefer to meet his output and cost targets through speed-up or cost-cutting change in work rules than through a long-term commitment of capital expenditure (point **e**). The worst outcome for each is to select High while the other selects Low. A high level of investment when the worker gives a low level of support of productivity-enhancing practices will lock the employer into an unprofitable operation. Similarly, for the worker, supporting productivity-enhancing practices while the employer invests little will lead to both exhaustion and job terminations.

The above strategies and outcomes are summarized in Figure 1.10, from which it can be seen that the employer–employee relationship in production is a prisoner's dilemma: For each, the *dominant strategy* (that is, the action that maximizes a player's payoffs regardless of what the other does) is to select Low, leading to the third-best outcome for both. The dismal third-best result occurs because the interaction is non-co-operative, in the sense that binding agreements between the two cannot be made. In the absence of such agreements, the more desirable outcome (High, High) is not sustainable: If by chance it occurred, each would have the incentive to defect to the Low option. Hence the high-productivity outcome cannot be sustained in this governance structure.

How might the collectively beneficial high levels of both investment and work be secured? The two (for simplicity, regarding the worker as a single actor) could agree to select

Employer investment level

		High	Low
Employee support for productivity	High	Person I's second-best (103) Person II's second-best (3) (point **c**)	Person I's best (104) Person II's worst (1) (point **e**)
	Low	Person I's worst (101) Person II's best (4) (point **a**)	Person I's third best (102) Person II's third best (2) (point **f**)

Figure 1.10 *Investment and productivity in a prisoner's dilemma*

High. Arriving at and enforcing an agreement of this kind would present serious obstacles under existing institutional conditions. Workers, for example, would require access to the firm's financial records, as well as a way of sanctioning the owners should they fail to comply. Owners likewise would require a low-cost and effective way of monitoring the work activities of the workforce. But monitoring is often exceptionally costly, if not impossible given the nature of the work process, and the difficulties are exacerbated by the unwillingness of workers to co-operate in such monitoring activities, since the employer is the residual claimant on the resulting income and hence the sole beneficiary of the effectiveness of the monitor and of the worker's efforts.

Suppose some agreement could be struck allowing the preferable outcomes **b**, **c**, or **d**. But which one? The answer will depend on the bargaining power of the two parties, and this, in turn, would depend on the consequences for each of failing to come to an agreement, or the so-called fallback outcome, point **f**.

In a bargaining situation, then, both persons have an incentive to avoid any move that worsens their fallback position.

Thus, the employer would want to avoid any type of fixed investments that cannot be relatively easily redeployed elsewhere, including, importantly, investments in the worker's own job skills. Workers, for their part, would want to avoid any simplification of the work process which would facilitate their own replacement. Hence, both workers and employers will direct their efforts towards activities that increase their expected share of the firm's net revenue. These activities may be very costly; they need not contribute to productivity, and typically they do not. Models of this process that show why efficient bargains are often not possible are provided in Bowles (2004).

To the waste associated with the bargaining process must be added the likelihood that in many cases no agreed-upon rule for sharing the benefits of co-operation will be adopted, therefore no agreement will be struck, and the productivity gains will be forgone. Or perhaps an agreement will be secured only after costly strikes or lockouts. Often no agreement will be struck at all, and the employer will simply offer the worker a wage high enough to make the job worth keeping, and then threaten to fire any worker who does not work sufficiently hard.

But such threats are ineffective unless the employer devises a system of surveillance of the labor process, deploying surveillance equipment and supervisory personnel around the workplace for this purpose. In actual capitalist economies, these monitoring costs constitute a considerable fraction of the cost of employing labor. (Supervisory labor is included in the guard-labor statistics presented in Figures 1.3–1.5.) Estimates vary, of course, but monitoring expenses broadly defined appear to be about one-fifth of the cost of labor in the US. The resources devoted to monitoring the labor process are of roughly the same magnitude as those devoted to producing the capital goods with which workers are employed (Gordon 1994).

Conclusion

No particular importance should be attributed to the specific workplace co-ordination failure I have chosen for purposes of illustration. A similar situation with analogous results could describe the worker's decision as to how much learning of firm-specific skills to undertake and the employer's decision as to how much employment security to grant workers, for example. Firm-specific skills contribute to productivity, but they are useless to a terminated worker, and hence there is little reason to acquire them in the absence of a job guarantee.

The example can be no more than a metaphor for the far more complex co-ordination failures resulting from the non-co-operative nature of the microeconomic interactions which determine the level of productivity and its growth. But the model is not misleading in its major conclusion: namely, that overcoming co-ordination failures often requires agreements which are difficult to secure and costly to enforce given the governance structures that are feasible when property rights are highly concentrated.

We turn therefore to the high cost of wealth inequality and the possibility that a redistribution of wealth would be productivity-enhancing.

2

The economic cost of wealth inequality

The claim that high levels of wealth inequality degrade economic performance by precluding what otherwise would be productivity-enhancing solutions to coordination problems sounds abstract. But this is not just blackboard economics.

In the US South prior to the Emancipation Act (1863) it was said that cotton was king. But it was not until after the Civil War that cotton truly ascended to the throne among crops: In the quarter of a century following the demise of slavery, the production of cotton relative to corn (the main food crop) increased by 50 percent (Ransom and Sutch 1977). The intensification of the cotton mono-culture puzzled observers at the time and since, as it coincided with a slight *downward* trend in the price of cotton relative to corn. Moreover, there were no changes in the technical conditions of production that would have offset the adverse price movement; in fact, the growth of corn yields appears to have outpaced cotton yields during this period. Nor can the shift from corn to cotton be explained by changes in factor supplies. The Cotton South experienced a serious labor shortage following the war, which should have led some farmers to abandon cotton in favor of corn, as the latter was a much less labor-intensive crop.

What then explains the growing dominance of cotton? To answer this we need to investigate the structure of local credit markets. To finance the crop cycle, most farmers – poor share croppers and rental tenants, many of these former slaves – purchased food (including corn) and other necessities on credit during the growing season. Because there typically was a single merchant in each locality, the goods prices at which the farmers accumulated their debt were inflated by the monopoly power of the merchant-lender. The loans were repaid when the crop was sold at the end of the season. Most farmers were too poor to post collateral, so the merchant-lenders secured their loans by means of a claim (called a lien) on the farmers' future crop in case of default. This *crop lien* system, according to its most prominent students, Roger Ransom and Richard Sutch, favored cotton:

> In the view of the merchant, cotton afforded greater security for such loans than food crops. Cotton was a cash crop that could readily be sold in a well-organized market; it was not perishable; it was easily stored ... For these reasons the merchant frequently stipulated that a certain quantity of cotton be planted ... It was the universal complaint of the farmers that the rural merchants predicated his willingness to negotiate credit on the condition that sufficient cotton to serve as collateral had been planted. (Ransom and Sutch 1977:160)

The crop lien system that came to prominence in the post-Emancipation South was an ingenious solution to the problem of providing credit to asset-poor borrowers. It substituted the farmer's unenforceable promise to repay the loan in the future by an action observable by the lender *prior* to the granting of credit, namely having *already* planted cotton on which the merchant had first claim.

Taking account of the relative resource costs and prices of the two crops, Ransom and Sutch estimated that the cotton farmer purchasing corn on credit could have increased his income by 29 percent by shifting resources from cotton to corn. But this was precluded by the fact that, because the farmer had little wealth, he needed credit, and for the same reason, getting credit meant planting cotton. The result, according to Ransom and Sutch was that:

> The southern tenant was neither owner of his land nor manager of his business ... his independent decision making was limited to the mundane and menial aspects of farming. The larger decisions concerning land use, investments in the farm's productivity, the choice of technology, and the scale of production were all made for him. (Ransom and Sutch 1977: 170)

The fact that poor people are disadvantaged in credit markets also helps to explain a contemporary puzzle. Residential tenancy, like farming under absentee ownership, incurs inefficiencies typical of the coordination problems mentioned in the previous chapter. A residential tenant's maintenance of the property and civic actions to enhance the quality of the neighborhood environment contribute to the value of the owner's property, but cannot be specified in an enforceable contract. Thus tenants have little incentive to maintain the property and to participate in enhancing local amenities. Owner-occupied residences avoid the resulting incentive problems because the person taking the maintenance or civic amenities actions and the residual claimant on the benefits of these actions are the same individual, namely, the owner. Yet over a third of US families rent rather than own their home (Savage 1999), and in many countries the fraction is much higher. As an empirical matter, home ownership induces better care of the residence and also higher levels of participation in local government activities (Verba, Schlozman, and Brady 1995, Glaeser and DiPasquale 1999).

Why then is renting rather than owning one's residence so common, especially among those with low incomes? The answer is that renters do not have access to mortgage credit. In 1993, only 13 percent of renting families could secure a loan to buy even a low-priced home (one at the tenth percentile of homes ranked by price in the family's neighborhood [Savage 1999]). The remaining 87 percent of renters had too few net assets and too little income to secure a conventional mortgage.

Both examples – the triumph of King Cotton and misaligned incentives for the residential tenant – contrast sharply with the utopian world of complete and costlessly enforceable contracts that, until recently, was the standard assumption in economics. In this assumption, wealth conveys quantitative advantages – it determines the location of one's budget constraint – but all participants in the economy face the same contractual opportunities (and hence the same prices) irrespective of their holdings. The poor are constrained to buy less than the rich, but they transact on the same terms. By contrast, where contracts in financial markets are incomplete or unenforceable, individuals lacking wealth are either precluded from engaging in a class of contracts that are available to the wealthy, or enter into these contracts on unfavorable terms. Thus, wealth differences have political as well as economic effects, excluding some and empowering others.

The most obvious reason why an individual's amount of wealth influences the kinds of contract she can engage is that only those with sufficient wealth can undertake projects on their own account, that is, without borrowing. And among those who do borrow, those with more wealth borrow on better terms. This is because greater wealth on the part of the agent allows contracts which more closely align the objectives of principal and agent. This is the case, for example, when the borrower has sufficient wealth to post collateral or put her own equity in a project, and therefore has greater incentives to supply effort, to adopt the more prudent risk levels preferred by the lender (the principal), to reveal information to the principal, and to act in other ways that advance the principal's interests but that cannot be secured in a contract.

Those lacking wealth, for example, may acquire funds to support their education and other forms of human capital on less favorable terms than the rich and, as a result, may forgo investments in learning when private and social returns exceed their costs. Similarly, as we have seen in residential housing markets, those with sufficient wealth are more often owners and, therefore, residual claimants on the actions they take to improve the property and the neighborhood, while the asset-poor are more likely to be renters.

Thus, differences in wealth are reflected in distinct contractual opportunities: Those available to the wealthy are more likely to embody incentives supporting efficient outcomes, while those available to the wealth-poor do not, thereby imposing additional disadvantages on the poor. As a result, we will see, those without wealth often are precluded from undertaking highly productive projects from which they and others could benefit, or they are constrained to undertake these projects on a smaller than optimal scale, or to engage in contractual arrangements with sub-optimal incentive structures such as residential tenancy, sharecropping or wage labor.

While other financial markets are involved, the main analytical issues are best illustrated by the credit market, the subject of this chapter. I begin with a review of evidence on the extent to which people are excluded from credit markets or are *credit-constrained* (that is, they cannot borrow at all or as much as they would like at the current rate of interest). I then introduce the basic problem of incentives arising from the incompleteness of the contract between borrower and lender, and explore how the provision of equity or collateral by the borrower may attenuate these incentive problems. Next I embed the borrower–lender relationship in a model of general competitive equilibrium to show why prospective borrowers lacking wealth may fail to secure financing (or will be constrained to finance only small projects or to pay high rates of interest). The wealthy will be able to finance (and hence implement) projects that are larger and of lower quality than the projects that the poor are able to finance, and for identical projects the wealthy will pay a lower interest rate.

An important consequence is that because a lack of wealth may prevent an individual's high-quality projects from being implemented, the distribution of wealth matters for productivity. I then explore some implications for policy, examining the conditions under which an efficient distribution of property rights will occur through private exchange, and provide an example in which a redistribution of assets by fiat may generate positive productivity effects that (unlike the Chilean land transfers) are sustainable in competitive equilibrium.

Credit constraints: evidence

Much of the evidence about credit constraints (surveyed in Jappelli 1990) is based on the cyclical fluctuations of consumption, where the "consensus" estimates suggest that in the US about one-fifth of families are credit-constrained. These tend to be younger families with lower levels of wealth. These studies do not observe the borrowing activities of individuals and hence are somewhat indirect.

More direct evidence surveyed in Banerjee and Duflo (2010) is based on actual credit histories. Jappelli (1990) found that 19 percent of US families had their request for credit rejected by a financial institution; the assets of these credit-constrained families were 63 percent lower than the unconstrained families. "Discouraged borrowers" (those who did not apply for a loan because they expected to be rejected) had even lower wealth than the rejected applicants. Another study of US families (Gross and Souleles 2002) exploits the fact that credit card borrowing limits are often increased automatically. If borrowing increases in response to these exogenous changes in the borrowing limit, we can conclude that the individual was credit-constrained. The authors found "that increases in credit limits generate an immediate and significant rise in debt" (181). Gross and Souleles' estimate of the extent of credit limits is as follows:

> It is plausible that many of the one-third of households without
> bankcards are liquidity constrained ... Of the two-thirds with
> bankcards, the over 56 percent who are borrowing and are paying
> high interest rates (averaging around 16 percent) might also be
> considered liquidity-constrained, lacking access to cheaper
> credit. Combined with the households lacking bankcards, they
> bring the overall fraction of potentially constrained households
> to over 2/3. (Gross and Souleles 2002:152–53)

Other studies are based on exogenous increases in wealth.
Blanchflower and Oswald (1998) found that an inheritance of
$10,000 doubles a typical British youth's likelihood of setting
up in business. In another British study, Holtz-Eakin,
Joulfaian, and Rosen (1994) found an elasticity of self-
employment with respect to inherited assets of 0.52, and that
inheritance leads the self-employed to increase the scale of
their operations considerably. Another study, Black, de Meza,
and Jeffreys (1996) found that a 10 percent rise in value of
collateralizable housing assets in the UK increases the number
of start-up businesses by 5 percent. Evans and Jovanovic
(1989) found that among white males in the US, wealth levels
are a barrier to becoming entrepreneurs, and that credit constraints typically limit those starting new businesses to capi-
talization of not more than 1.5 times their initial assets: "most
individuals who enter self-employment face a binding liquidity constraint and as a result use a sub-optimal amount of
capital to start up their businesses" (810).

A study of Italian households found that those who did
not borrow either because they were denied credit or believed
they would be refused credit were more likely to be larger,
poorer families, headed by an unemployed, less well-educated
woman (Guiso, Jappelli, and Terlizzese 1996). Moreover, in
comparison with families unlikely to face credit constraints,
poorer, younger families with more uncertain sources of
income (self-employment rather than pensions, for example)
tended to avoid holding risky assets, consistent with the
view that credit-constrained individuals enjoy lower expected

returns on the investments they do make. Asset-poor people in the US frequently take out short-term "payday loans" against their pay checks. In Illinois, the typical short-term borrower is a low-income woman in her mid-30s ($24,104 annual income), living in rental housing, borrowing between $100 and $200, and paying an average annual rate of interest of 486 percent (Vega 1999).

Several studies have shown that asset-poor people in developing countries may be entirely shut out of credit markets and also excluded from labor or land rental contracts with incentives that elicit high effort. Laffont and Matoussi (1995), for example, show that credit constraints limit the kinds of contract that poor Tunisians may engage in, substantially reducing their productivity and hence their incomes. Other studies in low-income countries show that individuals' wealth strongly affects farm investment, and low wealth entails lower return to independent agricultural production (Rosenzweig and Binswanger 1993). For example, Rosenzweig and Wolpin (1993) showed that poor and middle-income Indian farmers could substantially raise their incomes were it not for credit constraints: Not only did they underinvest in productive assets generally, but the assets they did hold were biased towards those they could sell in times of need (bullocks) and against highly productive equipment (irrigation pumps) which had little resale value. Similarly, Rosenzweig and Binswanger (1993) found that a hypothetical standard deviation reduction in weather risk (the timing of the arrival of rains) would raise average profits by about one-third among Indian farmers in the lowest wealth quartile, and virtually not at all for the top wealth holders. This evidence suggests that the wealthier farmers pursued riskier strategies with higher expected returns. The lack of insurance and restricted access to credit not only reduced the poor's incomes, it also increased the level of income inequality associated with a given level of wealth inequality.

Consistent with the hypothesis that the poor are credit-constrained is the strong inverse relationship between individual incomes and individuals' degree of impatience, termed the *rate of time preference*. Hausman (1979) estimated rates of time preference from individual US buyers' implicit trade-offs between initial outlay and subsequent operating costs in a range of models of air conditioners. (By law operating cost must be listed along with the price.) He found that while high-income buyers exhibited implicit rates of time preference in the neighborhood of the prime rate, buyers below the median income level exhibited rates five times this rate (they bought cheaper air conditioners that were more expensive to operate). Green, Myerson, Lichtman, Rosen, and Fry (1996) elicited rates of time preference from high- and low-income respondents in the US using a questionnaire method. The low-income group's estimated rates were four times those of the high-income group. In both the Green *et al.* and the Hausman studies, a 10 percent increase in the income of an individual was associated with about a 10 percent reduction in the rate of time preference.

Thus, there is considerable evidence that those lacking wealth are credit-constrained and face unfavorable opportunities in financial markets, as well as other restrictions on the kinds of contract in which they may engage. The resulting allocative inefficiencies appear to be substantial. The following model explains why this is so.

Borrowers and lenders

The promise to repay a loan is not generally enforceable for two reasons: The borrower may not have the funds sufficient for repayment when the repayment is due, and the borrower's choice of a risk level for a project is not generally subject to enforceable contracts. When an agent who lacks sufficient wealth has a "project" for which the level of risk is chosen by the agent, a standard principal–agent problem arises. An example follows, beginning with the (Robinson Crusoe) case,

in which no co-ordination failure occurs because the operator of the project is wealthy enough to finance it himself. This
will be followed by a case in which the same result occurs,
but for a different reason: Complete contracting is assumed.
These two cases establish the normative baseline for comparison with the more realistic cases where the operator of the
project is not sufficiently wealthy to finance it and hence
must borrow, and where borrowing contracts are incomplete.

For now, accept the unrealistic assumption that all actors
are *risk-neutral*, meaning that all they care about is the
expected returns on the project, not the variance of the returns,
so that the actor would be indifferent between a project that
yielded $100 with certainty and a fifty-fifty chance of yielding
either $50 or $150. A project requires $1 to carry out, and will
fail with probability f. Imagine that the "project" is a machine,
which, if it does not "fail," has a one-period life (it becomes
worthless at the end of the period) and which produces goods
in proportion to the "speed" at which it is run. For simplicity,
assume the speed is equal to the probability that the machine
will break (i.e. fail) or f. The goods produced are available only
at the end of the period under the condition that the machine
has not failed. (The machine will be worth nothing at the end
of the period whether it fails or not, but if it fails it also destroys
any goods it has produced as well.) The project returns μf if it
succeeds and 0 otherwise (μ is a positive constant), so the
expected returns net of all (non-interest) costs are:

$$r = \mu f (1 - f)$$

While the amount produced (if the machine does not fail) rises
with f, the expected returns reach a maximum beyond which
the higher output in the success state is offset by the greater
likelihood of a failure and zero return. Therefore the net returns
function has an inverted-U shape. The expected returns function abstracts from the opportunity cost of the investment,
which is $1 + \rho$ (had the owner not bought the machine and

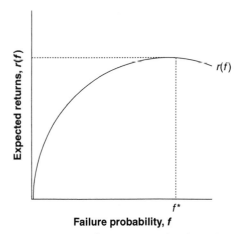

Figure 2.1 *The project technology.* Expected returns depend on the speed of the machine and hence on the degree of risk; and there is a level of risk that maximizes expected returns.

instead invested the $1 it cost at the risk-free interest rate ρ, he would have had $1 + \rho$ at the end of the period).

The Robinson Crusoe case. (See Figure 2.1.) A single owner of the (self-financed) project would vary f to maximize expected returns and thus would set $dr/df = \mu(1 - 2f) = 0$, the solution to which is $f = \frac{1}{2}$. To be viable, the project must return at least $1 + \rho$, and therefore the productivity of the project must be such that $\mu \geq 4(1 + \rho)$. (This is because the expected return on the project when f is optimized [set at $\frac{1}{2}$] is $\mu(\frac{1}{2})(\frac{1}{2})$.)

Fully contractible case. An agent (who I will call A) borrows the funds ($1) from a lender, the principal (P), at interest rate $\delta - 1$. At the end of the period, A repays P the amount δ (namely, the principal plus interest) with probability $(1 - f)$ and 0 otherwise. The assumption that the borrower repays nothing if the project fails is crucial to what follows. It reflects the common institution of *limited liability*; if the project fails,

the lender may not take the borrower's house. Therefore the
agent's per period expected return is:

(1) $y(f, \delta) = \mu f (1 - f) - \delta (1 - f) = (\mu f - \delta)(1 - f)$

Assume the agent's next-best alternative is to receive zero; so
A must expect to receive $y \geq 0$ in order to be willing to participate (this is A's *participation constraint*). If f is known to P and
is fully contractible, then P can simply offer A a contract such
that $y = 0$, thereby satisfying A's participation constraint as an
equality. Using the fact that the participation constraint is $(y = 0$
in equation [1]), we see that A's "supply price of f" (assuming
$f > 0$) is just $\delta / \mu = f$, a lower interest rate buying a reduced
probability of failure. Note that if this supply price is offered
(i.e. if P contracts for f according to $\delta = f\mu$), the agent will be
indifferent to any particular level of f, all of them resulting in
zero expected gain. The principal then varies f to maximize his
expected returns:

(2) $\pi = \delta (1 - f)$

which, substituting in the "price of f," gives:

$\pi = f \mu (1 - f)$

When the principal chooses f to maximize this expected
profit function, he will set $f^* = \frac{1}{2}$.

Figure 2.2 illustrates this case. The slope of P's iso-return
schedule is $(1 - f)/\delta$ and, at P's solution to the above optimizing problem, it is tangent to A's participation constraint, the
slope of which is $1/\mu$. Having determined the optimal failure
rate, the principal then uses the supply price of f to determine
the optimal interest rate to offer the agent, namely $\delta^* = \mu/2$. P
then offers A the following contract: A agrees to implement
$f^* = \frac{1}{2}$ and agrees to pay P an amount $\delta^* = \mu/2$ (which will
occur with probability $\frac{1}{2}$), satisfying A's participation constraint and giving P an expected gain of $\delta (1 - f)$ or $\mu/4$.

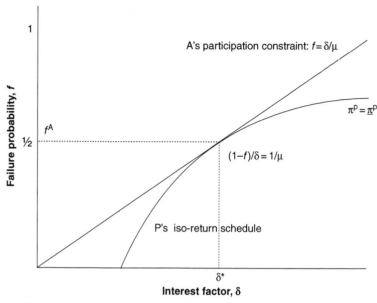

Figure 2.2 *A utopian credit market: The complete contracts case.* It is utopian because it assumes that the promise to repay is enforceable even if the borrower does not have the funds.

Note that the level of risk implemented is identical to that chosen by Robinson Crusoe. The reason is that the principal's objective function under complete contracting is the same as Robinson Crusoe's. (The same result would have held had we assumed that the promise to repay is enforceable but that f is not subject to contract.)

If you'd like a brief philosophical interlude, think about what just happened: We found that because the relevant contract was complete, what looked like a strategic interaction between two individuals (the principal and the agent) turned out to have exactly the same outcome as if there had been just a single person (Robinson Crusoe). As a result of the complete contract assumption, economics can be reduced to the parable of Robinson musing to himself about how much he should fish today, or whether it is time to repair his raft, and all of the other trade-offs that he faces in dealing with nature.

But there is more. Because in the case of complete contracts the participation constraint is binding, the lender was effectively maximizing profits subject to a constraint given by the borrower's utility level (her participation constraint) and therefore *by definition* implementing a Pareto-efficient outcome. The solution to this problem is obviously an outcome such that the lender could not be made better off without the borrower becoming worse off.

The same reasoning applies in other markets, including the employer–employee interaction in the labor market. Complete contracting not only erases the distinction between principal and agent, it also insures that the resulting allocation of resources will be Pareto-efficient. Maybe this is why Crusoe made so many appearances in nineteenth-century economics texts. The results change when we turn to real-world credit contracts.

Non-contractible risk, no collateral: In this case, f is not subject to contract, so the *agent* will choose f to maximize expected returns (which remain as before) by setting:

$$dy/df = \mu(1 - 2f) + \delta = 0$$

which, solving for f, gives the agent's best-response function:

(3) $f(\delta) = (\delta + \mu)/2\mu = \frac{1}{2} + \delta/2\mu$

The principal's expected profits are as before, but f now depends on δ, giving the principal's expected profit function:

(2′) $\pi = \delta(1 - f(\delta))$

Varying δ to maximize this function gives us the principal's first-order condition:

(4) $(1 - f)/\delta = f'$

which, using (3), gives the solution:

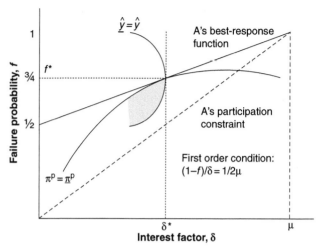

Figure 2.3 *The credit market with non-contractible risk.* In this non-utopian credit market the lender can neither enforce repayment of the loan if the machine fails nor can he control the speed at which the lender runs the machine and hence its risk of failure. As a result , the borrower chooses a probability of failure equal to 3/4 rather than 1/2 as in the utopian case. The shaded area shows combinations of the f and δ which both the borrower and lender would prefer; but they are not attainable because they are not on the borrower's best response function.

(5) $\delta^* = \mu/2$

and substituting (5) back into (3) gives $f^* = \frac{3}{4}$.

The agent therefore implements a higher level of risk than in the complete-contracting or Robinson Crusoe cases. Figure 2.3 illustrates the difference. Note the difference between A's participation constraint and A's best-response function (this explains the difference in the level of risk chosen by A). As a result, the borrower's expected income is positive (because the best-response function is above the participation constraint), and thus the borrower is receiving a rent. Returns to P are correspondingly lower: Substituting f^*

Table 2.1 *Credit market results for the case where the borrower has no wealth.* In the table 'na' signifies 'not applicable' and '(pc)' means 'participation constraint'

Case	agent's best response f^* $(\delta;\mu)$	risk f^*	interest factor δ^*	expected payoffs (y, π) **per period**
1. Robinson Crusoe	na	$\dfrac{1}{2}$	na	$\mu/4$ (to Crusoe)
2. Contractible risk	$f = \delta/\mu$ (pc)	$\dfrac{1}{2}$	$\mu/2$	$0, \mu/4$
3. Non-contractible risk	$f = \frac{1}{2} + \delta/2\mu$	$\dfrac{3}{4}$	$\mu/2$	$\mu/16, \mu/8$

and δ^* into the expression for π gives $\pi = \mu/8$ (rather than the expected profits of $\mu/4$ in the complete contracting case).

The *joint surplus* (the payoffs to the borrower and lender combined) is less under the incomplete contracts: With complete contracts the lender received $\mu/4$ and the borrower nothing, with incomplete contracts the lender gets $\mu/8$, as we have seen, and the borrower $\mu/16$. (Table 2.1 presents a summary of the results.) The Nash equilibrium allocation (f^*, δ^*) is also Pareto-inefficient. This can be seen in Figure 2.3. Compared to the outcome (f^*, δ^*) the lender prefers any point below the iso-return locus labeled $\pi^P = \underline{\pi}^P$ while the borrower prefers any point to the left of the iso-expected income locus labeled $\hat{y} = \hat{y}$. Thus, the points in the shaded area in the figure are Pareto-improvements over the Nash equilibrium.

Note the borrower's (or agent's) fallback position equals zero, but in the absence of complete contracting the borrower receives a *rent*, that is, a payment greater to her next-best alternative. This is not because the agent anticipates losing the rent in subsequent periods (remember, it is just a single-period interaction). It occurs because A responds adversely to higher interest rates, and the only way P can implement the profit-maximizing incentives is to offer the agent a transaction superior to her next-best alternative. In this case the rent is an unintended by-product of the principal's limited options in designing a contract for A. Given that a rent will be offered in any case, the principal in the single-period case could induce the agent to take fewer risks and hence raise the lender's expected profits by converting it to a multi-period contract. In the multi-period case (studied in Bowles 2004), the lender has authority over the borrower: He can threaten to withdraw the borrower's rent, and this threat induces the borrower to act in ways advantageous to the lender. The excess of the present value of the borrower's transaction over the borrower's next-best alternative is thus an example of an *enforcement rent*, namely a payment by a principal to enforce behavior on the agent that will benefit the principal.

Wealth constraints and credit-market exclusion

Suppose the agent has two types of income-earning asset. Human capital in the form of skills, schooling, and health is a source of earnings, but cannot be used as equity or collateral in a loan contract. The same is true of many homes and even land in many poor countries in cases where the poor owners of these assets do not have valid property titles. By contrast, most forms of material wealth may be used as equity or collateral. I will use the term "wealth" to refer to assets that may be used as collateral or equity.

Borrowers generally have some wealth, and if the project yields expected returns in excess of the risk-free interest rate it will be in the borrower's interest to invest in the project. There are two reasons why investing one's own wealth in a project may be in the interest of the borrower, corresponding to the two sources of incentive problems in principal–agent relationships, namely, hidden attributes and hidden actions. First, if, contrary to our assumption, the lender does not know μ, investment of the borrower's own wealth is a credible signal of the borrower's assessment of the quality of the project. Someone with a low μ project (a not-so-good machine) would be unlikely to invest his or her own assets. As we will see presently, in competitive equilibrium those with less wealth will need superior projects to obtain financing, so the borrower has an interest in overstating a project's quality in order to secure a loan. This is the *hidden-attribute* case. The second reason, and the one modeled here, is that the discrepancy between the objectives of the lender and borrower concerning the choice of the level of risk (this is the *hidden action*) would be attenuated if the borrower invested in the project and, thus, shared some of the risk of failure with the lender. In what follows I use the terms "wealth" and "level of equity committed to the project" interchangeably: Agents devote all their wealth to the project, if they devote any.

Non-contractible risk with borrower's equity. Suppose the agent has wealth k currently invested in a risk-free asset yielding a rate of return ρ. Should the agent devote these funds instead to the risky project, he would then borrow only $1-k$, and the expected returns (including the opportunity cost of the forgone returns on the risk-free asset) would be:

$$y(f;\delta) = \mu f(1-f) - \delta(1-k)(1-f) - (1+\rho)k$$

The agent will then select f so as to maximize y, with the resulting first-order condition:

(9) $f(\delta, k) = \frac{1}{2} + \delta(1-k)/2\mu$

which is exactly as before, except for the $(1-k)$; as the equity share of the agent rises, the chosen risk level falls. As before, higher interest rates (δ) rotate the best-response function upwards, while superior projects (μ) rotate it downwards. Notice that as $k \to 1$, $f^* \to \frac{1}{2}$, so complete financing of the project by the agent reproduces the prudent and socially optimal Robinson Crusoe result, as one would expect. The lender, acting as first mover and varying δ to maximize expected profits (2′) subject to this best-response function (9), will select $\delta^* = \mu/2(1-k)$. The agent, responding according to (9), will choose $f^* = \frac{3}{4}$. (Substitute the expression for δ^* in the agent's best-response function (9) and you get $f^* = \frac{3}{4}$.)

The outcome, (f^*, δ^*), is an equilibrium for the interaction of the principal and agent in isolation: Both actors' first-order conditions for the relevant maximum problem are fulfilled. As a result (f^*, δ^*) is a mutual best response; neither could do better by unilaterally altering their action, making this outcome a Nash equilibrium.

Having analyzed the dyadic principal–agent relationship between lender and borrower, I now ask how it works out for the entire market, with many borrowers and lenders. To do this I embed the dyadic model in a competitive general equilibrium setting, using a short-cut. Rather than modeling the interactions of many agents, I introduce what is called a *zero-profit condition*. As there are many competing lenders, in equilibrium they all receive an expected return equal to the risk-free interest rate, ρ. (The expected profit rate according to this condition is not zero, making it something of a misnomer; "zero excess profits" might be a better term.) Thus, the expected wealth at the end of the period must be the same for those investing in the risk-free asset and those investing in the risky project, or:

$$(10) \quad \pi = \delta(1-f) = (1+\rho)$$

The basic idea expressed by the zero-profit condition is that, if expected profits exceed ρ, then money will flood into the market looking for borrowers. And conversely, if profits fall below ρ, then the supply of loanable funds will dry up. There is a lot to say about how such a zero-profit condition might come about. A simple but unrealistic story is that the rich have a rate-of-time preference equal to ρ, and that when π falls below this they eat their capital rather than loaning it (and,

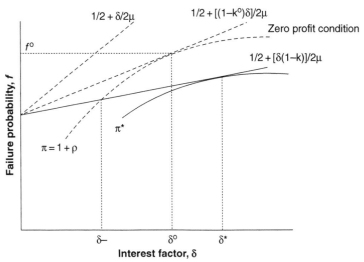

Figure 2.4 *The competitive interest rate and credit market exclusion.* The steeper dashed line is the best response function of the would-be borrower with no wealth. Every point on this function would yield the lender less than the opportunity cost of capital (the line is everywhere above the zero profit condition) so this borrower is excluded from the credit market. The solid line is the best response function of a wealthy borrower, with whom the lender is happy to do business.

correspondingly, when π exceeds ρ they seek out borrowers of their wealth). More realistically we could assume, as I do in the next chapter that the credit market in question is in a small nation whose financial markets are globally integrated and where loanable funds are reallocated around the world in response to differences in expected profits.

The condition that, in competitive equilibrium, profits not exceed the risk-free rate of interest defines a particular "iso-expected returns" locus in (f, δ) space labeled $\pi = (1 + \rho)$, as depicted in Figure 2.4.

Below this zero-expected profit locus (for lower f or higher δ) the expected rate of return exceeds the competitive risk-free rate, inducing wealth holders to supply more funds to the loan market. Above the zero-profit locus, funds will be withdrawn. Thus, the competitive equilibrium – where there is no change in the amount of funds loaned – must be at some point along the locus.

Think about some borrower whose wealth, call it k^o, is just enough that her best-response function is tangent to this zero-profit condition, with the outcome defined by this tangency designated in Figure 2.4 by the point (f^o, δ^o). Lesser levels of wealth give a best-response function lying wholly above the zero-profit locus, and hence there is no offer the lender can make which will generate an expected return greater than or equal to $1 + \rho$. As a result, borrowers with $k < k^o$ are unable to borrow. They are the *credit-market-excluded*.

What of borrowers with $k > k^o$? A best-response function for one such borrower (with wealth k) is depicted in Figure 2.4. Before turning to the competitive case, think about the determination of the interest rate and risk level for a non-competitive bilateral exchange, as might take place between an urban pawn shop or a "payday lender" and poor borrowers, or a small-town bank or money lender and his clients. In this situation, the lender is typically first mover, and he will maximize expected profits subject to the borrower's best-response function, and set $\delta = \delta^*$ as shown in the figure. If, on the other hand, the borrower is first mover (unlikely in the cases just mentioned), she will offer to pay $\delta = \delta^-$ which is the interest rate that (given the borrower's best-response function) gives the lender an expected profit rate just equal to the risk-free rate of return. Of course, any outcome with δ between δ^- and δ^* is possible, depending on the institutions governing the bargain.

In contrast to the bilateral case, suppose the institutions governing the interaction allow high levels of competition among lenders such that in competitive equilibrium each lender's expected profit is $1 + \rho$. Then the equilibrium transaction must be on the zero-profit locus. Because greater wealth rotates the best-response function downwards, it is easy to see that δ^- is declining in k for lenders with wealth $k > k^o$. As a result, the competitive equilibrium interest rate will vary inversely with the wealth of the borrower.

Wealthier borrowers will also be able to finance larger projects, and projects of lower quality. To see the first, let the size of the project, initially set at 1 now be $K \geq 1$, so k/K is the borrower's equity share. Now consider two borrowers, one with wealth of just k^o who can finance a project of size 1 paying δ^o, as above, and the other with wealth $k > k^o$. If the wealthier borrower's project were of size $k/k^o > 1$, then the best-response functions of the two borrowers would be identical. Both would then be offered δ^o, and as a result would select f^o, thus fulfilling the competitive-equilibrium condition. The result is that, with identical projects, the wealthier agent transacts at the same interest rate as the less wealthy agent, but is able to borrow more to finance a larger project and, hence, to expect a higher income. The less wealthy in this case are the credit-constrained: They can borrow, but are restricted to smaller amounts than the rich.

So far we have assumed that all projects are of equal quality, namely that μ did not vary among borrowers. Relaxing this unrealistic assumption will reveal another penalty imposed on the less wealthy. Assume that an agent unable to provide equity ($k = 0$) has a project for which $\mu = \mu^o$, and that a wealthier ($k > 0$) agent has $\mu^k < \mu^o$ (the poorer agent has a better project). To allow a comparison, suppose that both of them are marginal borrowers just able to finance their projects in competitive equilibrium, and hence that both pay the same interest rate. (In Figure 2.4, the best-response function for each is tangent to the zero-profit locus.) What do we know about the relative productivity of their projects?

A somewhat tedious calculation (Bowles (2004)) shows that:

(11) $\mu^k/\mu^o = 1-k$

If the wealthy agent can put up half the cost in equity, then her project can be half as good as the poor agent's (who can put up none). It is easy to see that had the poorer agent had some wealth available for equity, $k^o < k$, the above relationship would be:

$$\mu^k/\mu^o = (1-k)/(1-k^o)$$

which means that the minimal quality of a project required to secure funding expressed as a ratio among two prospective borrowers is proportional to the fraction of the project which cannot be self-financed.

We thus have three results in the competitive-equilibrium case: *for borrowers with wealth sufficient to secure lending to finance the minimal-sized project (K = 1), but not sufficient to self-finance the entire project, wealthier borrowers will be able to i) fund larger projects and ii) projects of lower quality; moreover, iii) for projects of the same size and quality as those of the less wealthy, the wealthier borrowers will pay lower interest rates.*

This, of course, cannot be efficient, as it implies that there will be some poor agents with good projects that will not be carried out, while some rich agents (and rich principals) will either have the wealth or be able to acquire it through borrowing to carry out inferior projects.

To see this, suppose that a total amount of finance is available normalized to be equal to 1, to be divided among projects (all of the same size) operated by a wealthy producer and one without wealth. Now rank the projects of each from the best (highest μ) to the worst, and assume that the projects will be financed in order of quality. Assume that the two borrowers have an identical distribution of project qualities. In Figure 2.4, the number of projects offered by the poor which

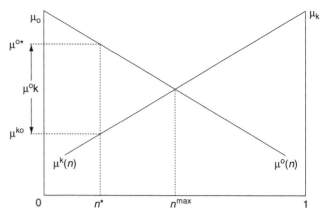

Figure 2.5 *Efficiency losses due to wealth inequality.* An efficient allocation of loans would be to provide n^{max} of funding to the borrower without wealth and the rest to the wealthy borrower so that the productivity of the marginal project of each would be equal. But a competitive credit market like that shown in Figure 2.4 will give more to the wealthy borrower, leaving the poor borrower with just n* of funding. The result is that the worst of the wealthy person's financed projects is less productive than the best of the poor borrower's excluded projects.

are financed is n, with $(1-n)$ the number of projects offered by the rich which are funded. We can write $\mu^o(n)$ for the quality of the nth project of the poor borrower and $\mu^k(n)$ as the quality of the rich borrower's worst-funded project when the poor borrower implements n projects. (Of course, if there were just a few projects, then the lines in Figure 2.5 would be step functions, but I assume that there are a great many very small projects, allowing the simpler linear representation in the figure.) The social optimum requires that no excluded project of either borrower be of higher quality than any included project. (Were there a large number of small projects, this would approximately equate the quality of the marginal projects offered by each.) In the figure, this optimum occurs when the poor gain finance for n^{max} projects.

But the competitive-equilibrium condition above (equation [11]) shows that the marginal project of the wealthier borrower will be of lesser quality than the marginal project of the wealthless borrower. Thus the poor will gain finance for only $n^* < n^{max}$. We can say more: Using the fact (from equation [11]) that for the marginal projects in competitive equilibrium $\mu^k/\mu^o = 1 - k$, we know that the difference in the returns on the marginal project, $\mu^o - \mu^k$, will be equal to $\mu^o k$. This is a measure of the extent of allocative inefficiency, and it is obviously increasing in k, the wealth difference between the two types of borrower. In this model, redistributing wealth from the rich to the poor (assuming its implementations were costless) would increase the social surplus: it would increase n^* and thus improve the average quality of projects.

Could such redistribution from the wealthy to those without assets followed by a compensation paid to the wealthy accomplish a Pareto-improvement, benefitting the poor without making the rich worse off? It is commonly thought that redistribution of wealth cannot pass the Pareto test for the simple reason that redistributions create losers as well as winners.

But this need not be the case if the redistribution is itself productivity-enhancing. To see this, refer back to Table 2.1. Suppose $\mu = 8(1 + \rho)$, so, in the case of non-contractible risk, the lender's expected profits $(\mu/8)$ is just equal to the risk-free rate of return, while the wealthless borrower's expected income $(\mu/16)$ is $(1 + \rho)/2$. Imagine (for dramatic effect) that at the start of some period the government confiscates the "$1 machine" required by the project from its rich erstwhile owner and gives it to the poor erstwhile borrower, who then operates it as did Robinson Crusoe. (Or the government could tax the rich lender $1 and give that to the poor.) At the same time, the government imposes a tax obligation on the beneficiary of this redistribution, requiring him to pay $1 + \rho$ at the end of the period (if the project fails, he will have to pay the tax from the earnings on his human capital). The beneficiary's expected payoff before paying the tax would be the same as Crusoe's, namely $\mu/4$, which, given the assumed value of μ, is $2(1 + \rho)$. If the beneficiary received this amount, he could pay his tax obligation, which the government would then use to compensate the erstwhile owner, paying the latter his expected return as owner $(1 + \rho)$. The beneficiary of the redistribution would retain an expected amount of $(1 + \rho)$ for himself, and thus be better off as a result. (Recall he made only half this amount as a borrower.)

The redistribution of wealth made the poor better off without affecting the income of the rich. Was there a trick? There is nothing special about the numbers. All that is required is what must be the case, namely that the total expected surplus is larger in the owner-operator (Crusoe) case.

If a Pareto improvement is possible, you may wonder why the owners of the machines do not just lease them to the poor in return for a promise to pay the owner a rent of $1 + \rho$ at the end of the period. But this transaction simply replicates the incentive problems encountered in the loan contract, for the promise to pay the rent is unenforceable. The government addressed this problem by extracting the compensation from the beneficiary *irrespective of the fate of the project* (the government *can* take your house), essentially offering an *enforceable* loan contract to the beneficiary at the risk-free interest rate. What the asset transfer plus the tax accomplishes is to turn the new owner-operator of the project into a Robinson Crusoe, the residual claimant on all of the risk entailed by his choices. It is this that accounts for the allocational superiority of the Robinson Crusoe case and allows for the seemingly anomalous *Pareto-improving egalitarian redistribution*. You still suspect it's too good to be true. Why wouldn't governments routinely undertake such win-win confiscations? It is time for some bad news.

Risk aversion, ownership, and allocative efficiency

To see why it may be impossible to implement Pareto-improving redistributions or why such redistributions, if implemented by fiat, might be welfare-reducing even for its purported beneficiaries, we need to make the above model more realistic. We have assumed that all parties are risk-neutral. Yet there is good evidence that the poor are risk-averse and that risk aversion is decreasing in an individual's income level (Binswanger 1980, Saha, Shumway, and Talpaz 1994). Thus, the poor may prefer share-cropping or wage employment because these contracts shield them from risk, even if their expected incomes would be higher as residual claimants. This is the lesson of the Chilean land reform.

We thus need to answer two questions. First, under what conditions will the relatively poor prefer to hold rights of control and residual claimancy over productive assets that are exposed to risk? And second, does there exist a class of redistributions that enhances productivity, that would not come about through voluntary contracting, and yet would be sustainable as competitive equilibria were such redistributions to be implemented by fiat? Answering these questions will require some new tools.

If an individual's utility as a function of her income is $U = U(y)$, then the so-called *Arrow-Pratt measure of risk aversion* is a measure of the concavity of the utility function, that is, the rate at which the marginal utility of income diminishes as income increases. This is the ratio of the second to the first derivative of the utility function (with a minus sign in front): $\lambda = -U''/U'$. The denominator is just the marginal utility of income, and the numerator is the rate of diminishing (utility) returns to income.

If the utility function is less concave at higher levels of income, or $d\lambda/dy < 0$, then *decreasing risk aversion* is said to obtain. While the concavity of the utility function undoubtedly captures important aspects of behavior in the face of risk, it certainly misses important influences on behavior, such as aversion to uncertainty, ambiguity, fear of the unknown, and so on. I will here introduce a framework that regards the concavity of the utility function as one of many reasons to wish to avoid risk. The approach captures the Arrow-Pratt logic under appropriate conditions, but is not restricted to it. The basic idea is to represent expected income as a good and the variance of income as a "bad."

Suppose an individual's income, y, varies in response to stochastic shocks according to:

$$(12) \quad y = z\sigma + g(\sigma)$$

where $g(\sigma)$ is expected income and z is a random variable with mean zero and unit standard deviation. Thus, σ is the standard deviation of income, a measure of risk. States among which the individual must choose differ in the degree of risk to which the individual is exposed, σ. The choice of σ may refer to a technology choice, like the "speed of the machine" or the choice of high-risk, high-yield seed varieties over low-risk, low-expected-yield seeds. Or it might refer to a human capital investment choice such as the degree of specialization – a particular branch of engineering or liberal arts, for example – the more specialized education or yielding higher expected returns (over some range), but also incurring greater risks. Risk-return schedules of this type have also been estimated with respect to bio-diversity, with greater diversity being a hedge against variations in weather and other environmental influences. (Chapter 4 considers the political attitudes towards globalization and the welfare state among individuals who have human assets of varying degrees of risk exposure.)

The beauty of formulating risk as in equation (12) is that we can then write the individual's utility function as:

$$(13) \quad v = v(g(\sigma), \sigma)$$

with $\partial v / \partial g \equiv v_g > 0$ (expected income is a good) and $\partial v / \partial \sigma \equiv v_\sigma \leq 0$ (risk exposure is a bad, or at least not a good). This function expresses the individual's positive valuation of higher levels of expected income and negative valuation of more uncertain income, without implying that the latter is due to the concavity of the function $U(y)$. Because of the particular way I have introduced risk, however, this function is also able to capture the logic of the Arrow-Pratt measure (the general utility function $U(y)$ can be expressed as a simple two-parameter utility function in this case, because the variation in income is generated by what is termed a linear class of disturbances). The technical details are in Bardhan, Bowles, and Gintis (2000), drawing on the earlier work of Meyer (1987) and Sinn (1990).

The indifference loci representing an individual with decreasing Arrow-Pratt risk aversion appear in Figure 2.6. They are increasing and convex in σ, flat at the vertical intercept ($\sigma=0$), become flatter for increasing g when $\sigma > 0$ and become steeper for increasing σ. The slope of an indifference locus, $-v_\sigma/v_g \equiv \eta$ is the marginal rate of substitution between risk and expected income. Thus $\eta(g,\sigma)$ is a measure of the level of risk aversion experienced by an individual faced with a given level of expected income and risk. It is clear that this measure of risk aversion is increasing in the level of risk exposure. The vertical intercept of each locus is the *certainty equivalent* of the other points making up the locus: It gives the maximum amount the individual would pay for the opportunity to draw an income from a distribution with the mean and dispersion given by each of the other points on the locus.

Just as with the speed of the "machine" (and for the same reasons) it is plausible to assume that the so-called risk-return schedule, $g(\sigma)$, is inverted u-shaped, first rising and then falling as shown in the figure.

The decision-maker faced with this risk-return schedule will vary σ to maximize u subject to $g = g(\sigma)$ and thus will equate:

(14) $g' = -v_\sigma/v_g$

requiring that the marginal rate of transformation of risk into expected income (the left-hand side, that is, the slope of the risk-return schedule) be equated to the marginal rate

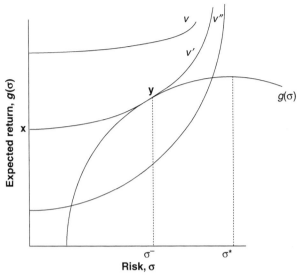

Figure 2.6 *Indifference loci of a decreasingly risk-averse person, and the choice of risk level.* The degree of risk aversion is indicated by the slope of the indifference locus at a given expected return and risk exposure. The indifference curves show decreasing risk aversion because they are flatter (less risk aversion) where expected returns are greater. A risk neutral individual would have flat indifference loci (meaning that all he cares about is expected returns), and would select σ^* as the risk level, earning a higher expected return than the risk averse individual shown, for whom σ^- maximizes her utility. Points **x** and **y** are on the same indifference locus but at **x** there is no risk, so point **x** is termed the certainty equivalent of point **y** and all other points on the indifference locus v'.

of substitution between risk and expected income (the slope of the indifference loci). A risk-neutral individual (namely, one for whom $v_\sigma = 0$) simply will set $g' = 0$, maximizing expected income at $\sigma = \sigma^*$. The risk-averse individual (with $-v_\sigma > 0$) will select a level of risk such that $g' > 0$, which implies a lower level of risk, with a lower expected return.

We can now answer the first question: Under what conditions will an asset-poor agent prefer to be the owner-operator rather than a wage worker on the same project? Assume there is an infinitely lived project generating the income stream described in (12), and requiring capital of amount κ to implement, the per period opportunity cost of which is just the risk-free interest rate, ρ. If the project is operated by an employee who is not the residual claimant, the owner must pay supervision costs m and pay a wage w to the employee, yielding the owner an expected profit of:

$$(15) \quad \pi(\sigma) = \sigma z + g(\sigma) - \rho k - m - w$$

Supposing that the employer is sufficiently rich to be risk-neutral, he will select $\sigma = \sigma^*$. Assume that competition among many similar employers imposes a zero (expected) profit condition, so that the equilibrium wage w^* is just high enough so that the expected profits equal the opportunity cost of capital, or setting $\pi(\sigma) = 0$ and rearranging (15):

$$(15') \quad w^* = g(\sigma^*) - \rho k - m$$

Would the employee receiving w^* with certainty prefer to be residual claimant on the uncertain income of the project, assuming that she could also select the level of risk? Let us first assume (contrary to the machine in the previous model) that the capital goods required can be rented for $\rho\kappa$ per period, or what is equivalent, that the erstwhile employee can borrow to purchase the capital goods required at the interest rate ρ. For simplicity, I also assume that as owner-operator the erstwhile employee expends exactly the same effort as before, but without incurring supervision costs. Then the owner-operator's income net of opportunity costs is:

$$(16) \quad y(\sigma) = \sigma z + g(\sigma) - \rho k$$

Writing the owner-operator's expected income as $\gamma = g(\sigma) - \rho\kappa$ gives the owner-operator's utility function $v = v(\gamma(\sigma), \sigma)$. Choosing σ to maximize this function requires, as before:

$$\gamma' = \frac{-v_\sigma}{v_\gamma}$$

Let the chosen risk level be σ^0, as shown in Figure 2.7, the two panels of which depict two situations which might occur with different prospective owner-operators whose levels of risk aversion differ (the one in Panel a is more risk-averse, as her indifference loci are steeper for any given combination of expected income and risk exposure).

In both panels, the risk-return schedule for the owner-operator is uniformly above that of the employer by the amount m, because in the former case self-employment obviates the need for supervision costs. But the risk-averse owner-operator selects a level of risk that is less than the expected

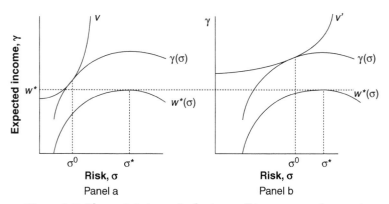

Figure 2.7 *The certainty-equivalent payoff to wage employment for a very risk-averse (Panel a) and less risk-averse worker (Panel b). The certainty equivalent of the risk-averse workers risk choice is less than the wage, so he would prefer to remain an employee rather than an owner; the situation for the less risk-averse worker is reversed, so she would prefer ownership to employment.*

income-maximizing risk level selected by the employer. In Panel a the certainty equivalent of the owner-operated outcome ($\gamma(\sigma^{o})$, σ^{o}) is less than w^{*}, so the individual would prefer to remain an employee rather than to assume the risk associated with residual claimancy. In Panel b the opposite is the case.

If the latter case obtained we would expect to see owner-operated projects rather than wage employment: Employees would acquire assets and become owners, implementing a Pareto-improving reassignment of rights of control and residual claimancy. This is exactly the insight underlying Ronald Coase's famous "theorem": Under suitable conditions, voluntary transfers of property rights should implement an efficient allocation, with residual claimancy and control of projects assigned to those who can operate them most productively.

But what makes this possible in our case is the unrealistic assumption that the owner-operator could rent the capital goods or borrow to purchase them at the risk-free interest rate. And we already know that the rate of interest will vary inversely with the ratio of the borrower's equity, k, to the size of the project, κ.

Suppose, then, that the interest cost of borrowing to acquire the asset (and the opportunity cost of devoting one's own wealth to equity for the project) is not ρ but, rather, is i, where:

$$i = i(k/\kappa) \text{ with } i' < 0$$

the expected net income for an owner-operator with wealth k is now

$$\gamma(k, \sigma) = g(\sigma) - i(k/\kappa)\kappa$$

The situation with this new risk-return schedule (labeled $\gamma(k,\sigma)$ for an individual with limited wealth is presented in Figure 2.8. Note that for the case depicted, the certainty equivalent of the individual's risk-return choice is less

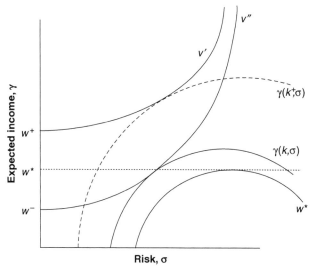

Figure 2.8 *Increasing the assets of the worker alters the choice of contract from wage work to ownership.* Without the asset transfer, the certainty equivalent (w⁻) is less than the wage w*. But by making the worker wealthier the asset transfer lowers both risk aversion and the opportunity cost of capital to the worker, so that the certainty equivalent w⁺ as a now-wealthier owner exceeds the wage.

than w^*. It is clear that the credit-constrained prospective owner-operator will prefer to remain an employee, even if, had she been able to borrow at the rate ρ, she would have preferred ownership. In this case, wage employment would exist in competitive equilibrium if employees had wealth of k or less (we assume that these non-owners would invest whatever wealth they had in an instrument with a return of ρ).

However, let's consider a policy that not only gives the worker ownership of the machine, but also substantially increases her wealth. We begin with an individual with wealth k and, as owner-operator of the machine, a certainty-equivalent utility of $w^- < w^*$, so remaining a worker would be preferable to owning the machine. But now suppose a redistribution of assets were to take place so that the employee had wealth k^+ greater than k. Her risk-return schedule (the dashed curve in Figure 2.8) would now give her a certainty equivalent greater than w^*. She would then be able to borrow at the rate ρ (or bear an opportunity cost of $\rho < i$ for the use of their own wealth in the project) and hence would become (and remain) an owner-operator. Both the pre-redistribution assignment of residual claimancy and control and the post-redistribution assignment are sustainable as Nash equilibria. Thus, a redistribution of property titles that would not have occurred through private contracting may be implementable by fiat and would persist following the redistribution as a competitive equilibrium without further government intervention.

Suppose that such a redistribution were accomplished by taxing wealth holders who, both before and following the redistribution, were risk-neutral and received a risk-free rate of return on their assets. If carried out without administrative or other costs, the redistribution would enlarge the total societal surplus: The opportunity cost of the assets forgone by those bearing the costs (namely, ρ) would fall short of the returns enjoyed by the beneficiaries (we know this because at an interest rate of ρ the employee would have preferred ownership).

The source of the efficiency gain is elimination of monitoring costs allowed by the substitution of self-employment for wage employment. This gain is partially offset by the reassignment of control of the risk choice from the risk-neutral erstwhile owner to a risk-averse owner-operator, coupled with the elimination of the insurance against risk enjoyed by the erstwhile worker that was provided by the assignment of full residual claimancy to the risk-neutral owner. As owner-operators they would therefore choose higher levels of risk and achieve higher expected incomes than would have been the case in the absence of the asset transfer. But it is implausible to think that any feasible redistribution could make the once-poor risk-neutral, so the effect of the policy would be to reduce risk-taking below the socially optimal level. The redistribution of wealth addresses the monitoring problem at a cost of giving up an efficient solution to the problem of risk (namely, let the wealthy risk-neutral former owner bear the risk). Where the former is a larger effect than the latter, efficiency gains result.

Of course, the redistribution is not Pareto-improving, as the wealthy would suffer a welfare loss. Despite the efficiency gains supported by the redistribution, it is difficult to imagine a feasible compensation for the losers, since the redistribution of assets was essential to generating the efficiency gains, and hence compensating the losers would require returning some of the wealth from the new owners to the erstwhile owners, which would reduce and possibly reverse the efficiency gains.

In fact, this reduced risk-aversion effect could induce erstwhile employees to become owners entirely independently of the reduced credit constraints effect explored above.

The hypothetical redistribution of assets is a vehicle for exploring the interaction of credit constraints, risk aversion, and ownership. It is not a policy design. Design of actual policies of asset distribution would need to address its administrative questions as well as general equilibrium and long-term dynamic effects not considered here. For example, will the once-poor adopt savings and investment strategies sufficient to preserve or enhance their assets? All the above analysis shows is that they would not prefer to sell the assets, should they acquire them at a cost of ρ or less.

The models presented in this chapter show why the asset-poor will pay higher rates when borrowing or be entirely excluded from credit markets. But there is a further conclusion: The asset-poor will have lower expected returns on their wealth. There are two reasons for this. First, those excluded from borrowing will have to invest whatever assets they have at the risk-free rate, ρ, which will be lower than the expected return on assets of those who are not excluded (except the marginal borrower). Second, less wealthy and hence more risk-averse individuals will select projects with lower expected incomes, as Figures 2.6 and 2.7 show. The prediction finds some empirical support in the US even for quite wealthy individuals and restricting the comparison to a given type of asset: The corporate stock held by high-income individuals appreciates substantially faster than the stocks held by less wealthy individuals (Yitzhaki 1987).

Conclusion

I conclude that where wealth disparities are so great that a small reduction in the assets of the rich would not preclude them from engaging in any technically feasible contracts, while granting additional assets to the poor would open up contractual opportunities for them, wealth redistribution can be a means of attenuating the incentive problems that arise in principal–agent relationships. This conclusion not only contradicts the message of the Coase Theorem that private transfers will insure that assets are owned by those who can make the best use of them. It also raises doubts about a staple in the folk wisdom of economics, namely the *efficiency–equality trade-off*.

The thrust of the above models presented here is not simply that wealth distribution may matter for allocative efficiency. To the extent that it does matter because it affects incentive problems arising from contractual incompleteness, it matters asymmetrically. More egalitarian distributions are likely to be more efficient. The reason is that it is the poor, not the wealthy, who are precluded from engaging in efficient contacts. If a particular asset would be more productive if the relevant rights of control and residual claimancy were in the hands of a wealthy individual, there are few impediments to this coming about through voluntary exchange. In these cases a competitive process will tend to assign property rights efficiently, as Coase said. The lack of a corresponding process in cases where an asset-poor individual would be the most efficient owner means that the needed remedy is to enhance the contractual opportunities of the asset-poor. Distributing assets to the poor can do this.

It is not difficult to think of exceptions to this statement. For example, concentrated wealth may allow the solution of collective action problems in the provision of public goods (Olson 1965). Thus, problems of monitoring corporate managers by owners would be attenuated if a few people were so wealthy that they owned entire firms outright (either because they are risk-neutral or have enough wealth to be sole owners and yet have a diversified portfolio [Demsetz and Lehn 1985]). While these exceptions are important, they do not add up to a compelling reason to doubt that egalitarian asset redistribution can enhance efficiency. The main efficiency gain allowed by concentrated wealth is that it assigns both control and residual claimancy to less risk-averse individuals, who then offer contracts providing the less wealthy agents with valuable insurance in the form of fixed-wage employment, crop shares, and other contracts that shield these risk-averse agents from income shocks.

The main drawback to this arrangement is that it requires that those performing non-contractible actions (work effort, for example, or, as in this chapter, risk-taking) not be the residual claimants on the consequences of their actions. Incentives to perform the action well are compromised as a result. Wealth redistribution addresses this incentives problem, but at a cost of reduced risk-taking. The static model used here fails to capture the long-term impact of a lower level of risk-taking. In a more appropriate dynamic setting, it could appear as a reduced level of innovation and as a result a lower level of long-term productivity growth.

This need not occur. A reduction in wealth inequality would directly counter some of these effects, as it would lower the barriers which now exclude many people from profiting by putting their new ideas into practice. Policies that encourage risk-taking have made small farmers highly innovative in many countries. Making the repayment of student loans contingent on one's subsequent income likewise provides insurance against downside risk. We will see in Chapter 5 that an unconditional basic income grant would also reduce risk exposure and promote risk-taking. A promising approach is expanded insurance against publicly observable exogenous shocks affecting the returns to one's productive assets (weather insurance for farmers, for example, or insurance pegged to exogenous price fluctuations for worker-owned co-operatives), or shocks unrelated to one's ownership of productive assets (health insurance, insurance against local variations in home prices).

But all of these fruitful avenues for the implementation of productivity-enhancing asset redistribution are clouded by a pervasive equality pessimism fuelled by exaggerated claims to the effect that globalization disarms the nation state as an agent of egalitarian redistribution.

3

Feasible egalitarianism in a competitive world

The word globalization had not been coined, but John Maynard Keynes sounded an alarm about its consequences that still resonates today:

> We each have our own fancy. Not believing that we are saved already, we each should like to have a try at working out our own salvation. We do not wish, therefore, to be at the mercy of world forces working out, or trying to work out some uniform equilibrium according to the ideal principles, if they can be called such, of *laissez-faire* capitalism ... We wish for the time at least ... to be our own masters and to be as free as we can ... to make our own favourite experiments towards the ideal social republic of the future. (Keynes 1933:761–2)

Few now remember Keynes' prescient advocacy of local self-determination and policy experimentation; but the tension between global integration and national sovereignty has become a staple of the conventional wisdom, endorsed by scholars and diffused by the media.

For well-known reasons, a reduction of impediments to international flows of goods and factors of production – commonly termed globalization – may enhance allocative efficiency both globally and within national economies, and the associated competition among nation states may contribute to governmental accountability. However, globalization is also thought to raise the economic costs of programs by the nation state to redistribute income to the poor and to provide economic security for their populations. Among the reasons is the fact that the more internationally mobile factors of production – capital and professional labor – tend to be owned by the rich, and a nation-specific tax on a mobile factor induces national-output-reducing relocations of these factors. Similar reasoning demonstrates the high cost of attempting to alter the relative prices of factors of production, for example, by raising the wage relative to the return to capital through trade union bargaining. Even Pareto-improving insurance-based policies are compromised, as cross-border mobility of citizens allows the lucky to escape the tax costs of supporting the unlucky, thereby reintroducing the problem of adverse selection plaguing private insurance, which (mandatory) public insurance was thought to avoid (Sinn 1997).

The result is a generalization of what Arthur Okun (1975) called redistribution in *leaky buckets*: the net benefit to the recipient may fall considerably short of the loss to those paying the costs. In a democracy, leaky buckets thus make it more difficult to secure governmental support for egalitarian redistribution, and thus compromise both the ethical appeal and the political viability of redistributive programs. By exacerbating the generalized leaky-bucket problem, trade liberalization and other aspects of globalization are thus thought to restrict the range of redistributive policy that is politically sustainable in democratic nation states. A leading mid twentieth-century international trade economist, Charles Kindleberger, concluded that:

> The nation state is just about through as an economic unit ... It is too easy to get about. Two-hundred-thousand-ton tankers ... air-buses and the like will not permit the sovereign independence of the nation-state in economic affairs. (Kindleberger 1969:207)

Recent treatments have echoed Kindleberger and advanced the position that global economic integration has sharply circumscribed the latitude for egalitarian redistribution by nation states. But is Kindleberger right?

Some of the more politically and economically successful redistributive policies – for example, Nordic social democracy and East Asian land reform– were implemented in small economies fully integrated into the global economy, which, on the above account, would seem to have provided a prohibitive environment for egalitarian interventions (Putzel (nd), Yang 1970, Yager 1980, Moene and Wallerstein 1993, Huber and Stephens 1998, Moene 1998). Other cases of egalitarianism in globally integrated economies include the Costa Rican welfare state (Rosenberg 1981, Mesa-Lago 1989, and Yashar 1995), the egalitarian distribution of health services and nutrition in Sri Lanka (Anand and Kanbur 1991, Isenman 1980), wage compression in Singapore (Lim 1984), and the public-health policies that dramatically reduced infant mortality under the socialist government of the tiny Seychelles Republic (World Bank 2011).

Particularly striking are the cases of two Indian states, Kerala and West Bengal. Goods and factors of production move freely across their boundaries, and their state governments have limited control over the legal and fiscal environment of their state economies. But investments in health, schooling, and other human capacities in Kerala and land tenure reform in both states (especially West Bengal) have substantially redistributed income and improved the well-being of the poor (Ramachandran 1996, Sengupta and Gazdar 1996, Banerjee, Gertler, and Ghatak 2002, Besley and Burgess 1998). The leftist governments credited with these policies were repeatedly returned to office in democratic elections (in the case of West Bengal over a period of three decades until their electoral defeat in 2011).

As even this brief description of cases of relatively successful egalitarian redistribution suggests, the reasons for the policies, as well as their designs and mechanisms, have differed substantially. Some owe their existence to electoral competition in polities with substantial majorities of poor voters; others have been implemented to forestall populist political successes. Each case exhibits serious shortcomings, but I will not dwell on these as my point is not to elevate them as models but rather is to make a modest claim: Unless these cases are entirely idiosyncratic, they suggest that the commonplace globalist variant of equality pessimism may be overdrawn (Bardhan, Bowles, and Wallerstein 2005).

To show that it indeed is, I present a model of globalization and redistribution seeking to answer the following question: In a globalized world economy, what programs of egalitarian redistribution and social insurance are implementable by democratic nation states acting independently? A program is implementable if its desired outcome is a stable Nash equilibrium of the appropriately defined game. An implementable program must therefore be economically and politically sustainable, that is, it must not be susceptible to being undone either by the electorate or by private exchange. (The Chilean land reform mentioned in Chapter 1 provides an example of an intervention that was undone by private exchange, and the contrasting case of the redistribution of assets to the erstwhile worker in Chapter 2 exemplifies an economically sustainable intervention.)

My response, drawing on recent work of many authors, is that in the absence of international co-ordination, globalization indeed makes it difficult for national states to affect the relative (after-tax) prices of mobile goods and factors of production, and for this and other reasons may limit the effectiveness of some conventional strategies of redistribution. But globalization does not rule out all egalitarian interventions. There remains a large class of feasible and sustainable governmental and other collective interventions leading to substantial improvements in the wages, employment prospects, and economic security of the less well-off. Included are redistributions of assets that are productivity-enhancing, namely those that provide efficient solutions to incentive problems arising in principal–agent relationships, such as wage employment, farm and residential tenancy, and the provision of environmental and social public goods in local commons situations. A review of these cases is provided in Bardhan, Bowles, and Gintis (2000).

The model I develop shows that these policies remain implementable in the above sense even in a hyper-globalized world, namely one in which investment responds instantaneously to between-country differences in the expected after-tax profit rate. This is not the world we live in, nor is it even a plausible approximation thereof (Glyn and Sutcliffe 1999, Taylor 1999, Bordo, Taylor, and Williamson 2003). But, given the widespread view that these aspects of globalization will thwart attempts at egalitarian redistribution, it is worth finding out if this is indeed the case, under admittedly extreme globalization assumptions. Whether the model illuminates real (if very long-term) tendencies operating in the world or alternatively is a more hypothetical exercise cannot be determined on the basis of existing empirical information. But even if it is only a hypothetical exercise, it is sufficient to indicate the faults of the globalist variant of equality pessimism, because recognizing that the world is really not all that hyper-globalized leads one to conclude that the purported constraints on egalitarian interventions are less stringent than I have represented them.

Globalization

To focus on the contribution of globalization *per se* to the leaky-bucket problem (and because the problems constituted by corruption and other forms of governmental malfeasance and unaccountability are well known), I will assume that governments are not self-serving leviathans, but rather seek to improve the living standards of the less well-off.

Because globalization is sometimes said to place particularly stringent constraints on trade unions, I will focus on the traditional concerns of organized labor: wages, jobs, and unemployment insurance. Redistribution thus will take the form of increases in the living standards of a homogeneous class of workers, either by raising their income or improving their prospects of being employed. Its focus is not on inequality *per se* but on labor-market outcomes affecting two important aspects of workers' well-being: jobs and pay. It abstracts from differences among workers and much else of importance, but seeks to explore the ramifications of two important empirical regularities. The first is that investment relocates globally in response to differences in expected after-tax profit rates, and the second is that, under a wide range of institutional conditions, real wages co-vary with the level of employment.

The basic assumptions of the model follow (the equations of the model are presented along with the notation in the appendix to this chapter see pp. 164–5). All markets are perfectly competitive, but labor (which is homogeneous within countries) is not mobile between countries. The global economy is thus modeled as if it were a national economy with a single capital market but segmented labor markets; the difference, of course, is that each labor market segment is represented by an autonomous government. There is a single good that is both consumed and used as capital (like corn: it is eaten and planted as seed). At the end of each period, after the payment of wages, wealth holders (those who own the corn surplus, if it exists) may either consume corn or allocate it as an investment good among many national economies in response to national differences in expected after-tax profit rates.

Actors differ by wealth level: the wealthy are risk-neutral, while those without assets (employed and unemployed workers) are risk-averse. Neither work effort nor the promise to repay a loan is contractible, so the relations between employers and workers and between lenders and borrowers are principal–agent relationships. Employers use monitoring and the threat of dismissal to induce workers to provide satisfactory levels of effort. For this reason (and perhaps others), the equilibrium of the labor market in each national economy is characterized by involuntary unemployment. (The underlying model is presented in Bowles [2004] and Shapiro and Stiglitz [1984]. It is extended to take account of aggregate demand in Bowles and Boyer (1988) and Bowles (2012).) Thus labor suppliers are quantity-constrained in labor markets: They cannot sell as much of their labor time as they would prefer at the going wage. Lacking wealth, they are unable to provide collateral or other means of attenuating the incompleteness of the credit contract. They are also excluded from credit markets or are credit-constrained for the reasons described in the previous chapter.

The competitive equilibria of this model for the single global markets in capital goods (corn) and credit support a common, global rate of expected after-tax profit and rate-of-time preference (and hence risk-free interest rate). By contrast, nation-specific institutions and cultures concerning labor relations, government policies, and security of property rights give rise to national differences in equilibrium wages and employment. There are thus $n+1$ prices in this model: Each of n nations' real wage (price of an hour of labor relative to the price of corn) and the global risk-free interest rate (price of goods now relative to goods later). As I will investigate just a single national economy, I will not give national subscripts to the relevant variables.

Because firms use a single production function and are otherwise identical, we can analyze production and wage-setting as if it took place in a single (competitive) firm. Aggregate output, Q, is simply total labor effort times average output per unit of effort, y, with a capital (seed) requirement of k per hour of labor. No production takes place if the total capital available, K, falls short of the capital requirement. Total effort is the average effort level per hour, e, of those employees (the directly productive workers) not engaged in monitoring multiplied by their hours of work, $h(1 - m)$, where h is the total (productive and monitoring) hours of work supplied in the economy, and m is the fraction of total work time accounted for by the monitors. Thus total effort supplied is $eh(1 - m)$, and the total capital required is $kh(1 - m)$, so:

(1) $Q = yeh(1 - m)$ for $K \geq kh(1 - m) = 0$

for $K < kh(1 - m)$

I normalize the national supply of labor hours at unity (given exogenously); so h (which varies between zero and 1) is the level of employment and $1 - h$ is the unemployment rate. Effort is determined by workers in response to the incentives and sanctions devised by the employer. As these include monitoring and the threat of job termination, the worker's optimal effort choice varies inversely with his or her fallback position, namely expected utility if employment is terminated. This depends on the expected duration of a spell of unemployment and the level of unemployment insurance or other income support that is conditional on being unemployed, b. Suppose effort may be either 1 (imposing a disutility of a on the worker) or 0, and that the probability of termination if $e = 0$ is τ. Then, with suitable simplifying assumptions (see the appendix to this chapter. pp. 164–166), the wage that will just induce workers to choose $e = 1$ equates the expected payoff of the two effort choices, which gives:

(2) $w^* = \dfrac{a}{\tau(1 - h)} + b$

as the "no-shirking wage." Equation (2) says that the wage that deters shirking will be greater, the more onerous the work is (larger a) and the larger the unemployment benefit is (larger b), and smaller, the higher is the probability of termination (τ) and the level of unemployment $(1 - h)$.

Of course, the termination probability (τ) and disutility of labor (a) depend on the institutional structure governing labor relations (the costs to the employer of firing a non-working employee, the perceived fairness of the wage determination process, the degree of effectiveness of the monitoring system, and the like). Along with $e = 1$, which it insures, the wage given by equation (2) maximizes both the firm's profits (offering a higher wage would serve no purpose) and the employees' utility (there would be no gain to shirking if the wage satisfies equation [2]). So the firm offering w^* and the worker supplying $e = 1$ is a mutual best response, that is, a Nash equilibrium. Thus equation (2) gives feasible combinations of w, h, and total effort supplied to firms; it is thus the *labor supply equilibrium condition*.

The model underlying equation (2) is quite particular, but it gives a convenient analytical form to the much more general empirical regularity mentioned earlier, namely $w_h > 0$, the fact that wages increase with the level of employment and also with the disutility of effort and the workers' fallback income b. For simplicity I assume monitors are paid the same wage as other employees, and I do not address the problem of their incentives to work. It will be important later to note that because employees do not shirk, they are not fired, and so bear no risk. There is therefore a group of $1 - h$ permanently unemployed.

Labor demand (and hence the level of unemployment) depends on the allocation of the global capital stock among national economies in response to differences in the expected after-tax profit rate. Recalling that the capital good is an intermediate input, the profit rate before tax is just total output minus the seed used up minus the wages paid (to all workers, including supervisors) or $(y - k)h(1 - m) - wh$ divided by the total capital stock, which, recall, is proportional to the number of productive (non-supervisory) workers, or $kh(1 - m)$. So:

$$r = \frac{(y - k)h(1 - m) - wh}{kh(1 - m)}$$
$$= \frac{y - k - w/(1 - m)}{k}$$

or (the second equation) expressed in per hour of productive employment by eliminating $h(1 - m)$ the profit rate is net output per hour of labor, minus the wage bill per hour of productive labor (that is, $w/(1 - m)$), divided by the capital input required to employ an hour of productive labor. Suppose that to finance its activities the national government levies a proportional tax on profits at the percentage rate t, so the after-tax profit rate is:

$$(3) \quad \pi = r(1-t) = \frac{(1-t)(y-k-w/(1-m))}{k}$$

Wealth holders finance a project if its expected return exceeds their rate of time preference, which I will assume is globally equal to the return on some risk-free instrument, ρ. Projects are exposed to a risk of "confiscation" or other unexpected reduction in their value, the probability of which, c (for confiscation), varies among countries, reflecting national differences in macroeconomic policy, political stability, criminality, and the like. Suppose the return is zero in the period of the confiscation: Wages are paid but the expected costs of contestation occasioned by the confiscation exactly exhaust the profits. The expected after-tax profit rate is thus $E(\pi) = \pi(1-c)$.

The national economy's level of corn investment is stationary (unchanging) if expected after-tax profit rates are equated across nations and are jointly equal to the risk-free interest rate or $E(\pi) = \rho$. This condition is akin to the zero-profit condition introduced in the previous chapter. Writing the insecurity premium $\mu = 1/(1-c) > 1$, this zero-profit condition becomes:

$$(4) \quad \pi = \rho\mu$$

Because r is monotonically declining in w, for a given country there is just one wage rate (call it $\underline{w}$) that will satisfy equation (4). If in some country $w > \underline{w}$, then the after-tax expected profit rate will fall short of the risk-free rate of return (the rate of time preference of the wealthy), and (given the hyper-mobility of capital) the country will receive no investment. Using equation (3) to rewrite (4), we find that this wage $\underline{w}$ is given by:

$$(5) \quad \underline{w} = \frac{(1-m)[y - k(1 + \rho\mu)]}{1-t}$$

When equation (5) obtains, the level of the capital stock, and hence employment, is stationary; it is the *equilibrium labor demand equation*, conditional, of course, on workers working $e = 1$. We need therefore to take the no-shirking wage into account, and doing this will determine the level of employment in the economy. Because $w^*(h)$ is monotonic, there is just one h consistent with $\underline{w}$. The general equilibrium of the national economy (taking ρ as exogenous) is defined by:

(6) $w^* = \underline{w}$

satisfying the condition for stationarity of both the employment rate and the wage rate.

To review, the causal structure determining this equilibrium has two parts. First, the nation's specific institutions and culture influence the net after-tax productivity of labor and the risk premium, which then jointly determine the national wage rate consistent with an unchanging capital stock given profit-maximizing by the owners of mobile investment resources (equation [5]). Second, the nation's institutions concerning labor markets and work organization determine what national level of aggregate employment makes that particular wage consistent with individual optimizing by firms and workers (equation [2]). Figure 3.1 illustrates the equilibrium of a given national economy (ignore the dashed curve for the moment).

Increasing wages and employment

Where, as in Figure 3.1, the equilibrium is unique and stable, the effect of country-specific policy interventions may be studied (as I will do presently) by means of a comparative static analysis of the displacement of the exogenous terms in $w^*(h)$ and $\underline{w}$. But the more complicated case of multiple equilibria (some of them unstable) cannot be ruled out. To see this, suppose that the confiscation probability c varies inversely with h – high levels of unemployment supporting a

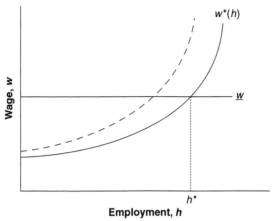

Figure 3.1 *Equilibrium employment and wages when capital is globally hyper-mobile.* The upward rising curve gives the lowest wage that will deter shirking by workers given each level of employment. The w function gives the wage rate that yields an expected after tax profit rate such that the countrys capital stock is constant, given the level of productivity of capital and labor, the required degree of labor supervision, the tax rate and the risk of confiscation.

populist or criminal environment, for example, so $\mu = \mu(h)$ with $\mu' < 0$. Then $\underline{w}$ is increasing in h, which (because w^* is also increasing in h) means that there may exist many values of h equating the two.

Figure 3.2 illustrates an upward-rising equilibrium labor demand function. There are two stable equilibria: **a**, the vicious circle of low employment, low wages, and a high insecurity premium ("Nigeria") and **a′**, the virtuous converse ("Taiwan"). The possibility of multiple stable equilibria enriches the policy analysis considerably, as it allows small one-time interventions to have permanent, non-marginal effects, and it provides a framework for analyzing possible divergent growth paths ("high road" vs. "low road" wage strategies, for example). A one-time demand expansion, for

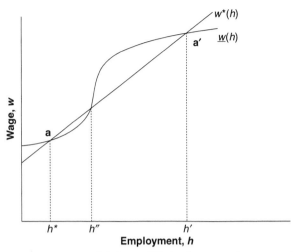

Figure 3.2 *Multiple equilibria due to endogenous risk.* At low levels of employment the risk of confiscation is substantial, so only a low wage rate allows a sufficiently high profit rate on capital that is not confiscated to avert capital flight. Higher levels of employment have the reverse effect, reducing the risk of confiscation and allowing higher wages while attracting capital.

example, pushing the employment level above the critical value h″ in Figure 3.2 could permanently shift the equilibrium from the low-wage and high-insecurity poverty trap to its virtuous converse.

The impact of strategies to raise wages and employment may now be assessed through their curve-shifting effects in Figures 3.1 or 3.2. For example, enhanced security of property rights, by reducing c (for any level of h) lowers μ, hence raises $\underline{w}$, and increases both h^* and w^*: Its effect is an increase in both wages and employment. From Figure 3.2 it can be seen that the upward shift in $\underline{w}(h)$ might also eliminate the "low road" equilibrium, displacing a national economy previously entrapped there to a rapid transition to the "high road."

The effects of changes in labor relations and labor market structure are equally transparent. Efforts to protect workers from dismissal for cause by reducing τ through job protection strategies shift the $w^*(h)$ function upwards (the dashed curve in Figure 3.1) without affecting $\underline{w}$, leaving the wage rate unaffected, but reducing employment. By contrast, reducing b, the magnitude of transfers whose availability is conditional on being out of work, has the opposite effect. Unlike a reduction in τ, which reduces welfare, the welfare implications of a decrease in b are ambiguous, as it lowers the well-being of the least well-off (the jobless), while reducing their numbers. The fact that protecting workers from dismissal would reduce worker well-being and a cut in unemployment benefits would increase employment will not be taken as good news among trade unions and leftist political parties: Both are results of the hyper-globalization assumption.

Trade unions may increase wages and/or employment in a number of ways, however (Bowles and Boyer 1990). First, unions may draw on workers' private information concerning the performance of other workers to improve the disciplinary environment of the workplace (raising τ or lowering m). Second, "union voice" effects (Freeman and Medoff 1984) may raise productivity and reduce the disutility of labor (the latter would lower the $w^*(h)$ function, supporting a higher level of employment). Third, collective bargaining agreements to provide well-defined job ladders and security from cyclical job loss provide greater incentives for firm-specific investments by workers (Pagano 1991). Both union voice and specific investment effects shift $\underline{w}$ upwards and $w^*(h)$ to the right. In a multi-period context, a reduction in the probability of job loss for reasons other than insufficient effort (protection from cyclical layoffs, for example) reduces the no-shirking wage because it increases the value of not shirking.

Fourth, negotiated incomes policies may lower or flatten the $w^*(h)$ function. Where, as in the Nordic social-democratic countries, especially Sweden, collective bargaining explicitly sought to implement wages consistent with successful competition in global markets, the $w^*(h)$ function came to approximate the $\underline{w}$ function itself (the latter defining the target wage in the bargaining model), with firm- and industry-specific wage drift accounting for discrepancies between the two functions.

Finally, $\underline{w}$ may become accepted as a fairness norm – perhaps because it is the wage rate that will give the employer a rate of return equal to what other employers receive, or to the marginal disutility of forgoing current consumption. Then, if, as seems likely, perceived fairness is a determinant of work effort, the $w^*(h)$ function will flatten, thereby increasing the employment gains associated with upward shifts in $\underline{w}$ due to productivity gains. Because, in equilibrium, no employee is working harder as a result of any of these changes, and because the unemployed prefer employment, the welfare gains associated with the implied trade-union-induced increases in wages and or employment are unambiguous. Thus, there is no shortage of trade-union-based policies that would improve the economic well-being of the employed, the unemployed or both.

The effects of government expenditures and the efficiency of public service delivery may be explored in similar fashion. Suppose the productivity of a unit of effective labor depends on λp, the effectiveness (λ) and level (p) of public expenditure on productivity-enhancing complementary inputs (such as nutrition, health care, schooling, and infrastructure) so $y = y(\lambda p)$ where the function y is increasing in its argument. Assume the government spends all of its tax revenues on p as well as b, the benefit paid to a worker when unemployed, giving the budget constraint (expressed as an equality) that equates the revenues spent on unemployment insurance and other public expenditure (the first and second terms on the left-hand side of the equation) with tax revenues (the tax rate t times total profits), or:

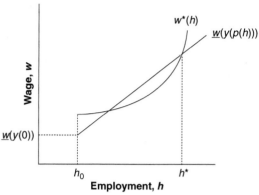

Figure 3.3 *Endogenous transfers and public investment.* Higher levels of employment allow a greater part of the public budget to be spent on productivity-enhancing investments (rather than unemployment insurance) thereby permitting a higher wage rate consistent with a constant stock of capital.

(7) $b(1 - h) + p = th((1 - m)y(\lambda p) - k - w)$

From (7) it can be seen that, for a given tax rate, there is a level of employment such that unemployment benefits exhaust the entire budget, and productivity per effective unit of labor is $\underline{y} = y(0)$.

Above this level of employment, however, productivity-enhancing public expenditures increase, which by equation (5) then requires a higher wage to equilibrate the capital market, yielding the upward-rising $\underline{w}$ function in Figure 3.3. The also upward-rising $w^*(h)$ function (as drawn) intersects the equilibrium labor demand function twice, suggesting a possible high and low public investment divergence among nations. (There is no "low road" equilibrium in this case, as h_o violates (6), while lower levels of employment violate the budget constraint.)

Because, for any level of h, w co-varies with λ and varies inversely with b, and because (as we have seen) decreasing b

also shifts the $w^*(h)$ function to the right, it follows that reallocating expenditure from transfers conditioned on unemployment towards productivity-enhancing public investment and increasing the effectiveness of public expenditures will simultaneously raise the (stable) equilibrium wage and employment level.

For a given level of b, λ, and h, there exists a tax rate that maximizes $\underline{w}$ (and hence both employment and wages); for obvious reasons it varies inversely with b (if taxes were spent only on b, the optimal rate would be zero) and co-varies with λ and h (where h is high, little tax revenue goes to unemployment benefits and more to productivity enhancement, so as long as the rate of return of public investment exceeds ρ it raises $\underline{w}$). It might appear that this change is unambiguously welfare-enhancing, but a more realistic model in which the employed periodically lose their jobs would show that for sufficiently high levels of risk aversion among workers, the lost unemployment insurance would more than offset the higher expected wage.

Increases in productivity (y), whether due to public expenditure or exogenous technical change, shift $\underline{w}$ upwards, allowing increases in equilibrium employment. But where productivity gains are shared with the unemployed through corresponding increases in b, the upward shift in the equilibrium labor supply condition $w^*(h)$ may reverse the potential employment gains. There is thus a policy choice concerning the manner in which productivity increases should be shared with the unemployed, through expanding the number of jobs on the one hand or by raising the average income of those remaining unemployed on the other.

As the examples in this section make clear, opportunities for raising wages and/or employment arise when allocative inefficiencies can be corrected either at minimal cost (as when union voice effects may attenuate the misalignment of incentives arising from the incomplete employment contract) or through expenditures on which the expected social rate of return exceeds $\mu\rho$ (as when credit constraints or other reasons induce workers to acquire less schooling than would maximize output per person). The problems of credit constraints and incomplete contracts may also be addressed more directly by a redistribution of assets or, more precisely, by a redistribution of the rights of residual claimancy and control commonly bundled with asset ownership, and by extending to the asset-poor the credit market and insurance opportunities of the wealthy.

Asset-based redistribution

To see how this might work, suppose that, at the beginning of each period, a national government borrows corn on the world market at the rate ρ and in turn offers to lend it to teams of members of production co-operatives at the rate $\rho\mu$, who at the end of the period are equal residual claimants on the income of the team, after repaying the government an expected amount of $1 + \rho$ per unit of corn borrowed. The simpler case in which, instead of teams of workers, individual producers use the corn to produce independently Robinson Crusoe-style is transparent, but not empirically relevant where team production is required by economies of scale or for other reasons. I assume that there is no rental market in corn. Assume that, should they be viable, these co-ops adopt a labor discipline strategy similar to their erstwhile employers' (dismissing non-performing team mates). Co-ops are therefore constrained to offer members a level of certainty-equivalent income $(\omega^*(h))$ equal to $w^*(h)$ in order to deter shirking. So a certainty-equivalent analogue to equation 2 must hold:

$$(2') \quad \omega^*(h) = \frac{a}{\tau(1 - h)} + b$$

Whether co-ops will form, and if they did, their effect on workers' income and the level of employment depends on the second equation – the labor demand equilibrium, giving the conditions under which the capital stock of the economy is unchanging – and this depends on how productive co-ops are compared with capitalist firms. Work mates have private information on each others' work activities, and, as residual claimants on the income of the co-op, team members are motivated to participate in mutual monitoring. As a result the monitoring costs that insure that a shirking team member will be detected is reduced to $m^- < m$. The monitors that the team members charge with the task of deterring shirking receive the same hourly payment as the directly productive co-op producers. (To keep things simple, I assume that the basic model of the capitalist firm is otherwise unchanged: tax rate on the use of capital (t), the confiscation risk premium (μ), and the likelihood of termination for a shirker (τ). Assets owned by workers might be less likely to be confiscated – for the same mutual monitoring reasons – thereby reducing the confiscation risk premium μ; but I will for simplicity confine attention here to the reduced monitoring cost of the co-ops.)

The co-op's advantage of reduced monitoring may be more than offset by sub-optimal risk-taking. The reason (as we saw in the previous chapter) is that risk-averse members now control the production process and (relaxing the assumption of given production technologies) face a choice among production methods of varying risk and expected output. Recall that as wage employees the producers bore no risk, but as residual claimants they cannot avoid risk exposure, given that they are residual claimants on a stream of output which is subject to stochastic variation.

Suppose that expected output per hour of effective labor is $y(\sigma)$, where σ is the standard deviation of output selected by the co-op members. For concreteness, imagine that corn may be planted at various times, and the expected return and its variance depend on the planting date, with greater risk being associated with higher expected returns over some range. Thus y is increasing and concave in its argument, reaching a maximum at

σ^* (the function resembles that in Figures 2.1 and 2.6). In the capitalist firm, the risk-neutral employer of course selected σ^*, so the analysis of the previous section assumed a level of expected productivity of $y = y(\sigma^*)$. But utility-maximizing risk-averse co-op members will select some level of $\sigma^- < \sigma^*$ and hence generate a level of expected income $y(\sigma^-) < y(\sigma^*)$. Co-op members are thus residual claimants on income stream generated by this lesser level of risk-taking.

Forming a co-op will be attractive to workers currently employed in conventional capitalist firms only if the certainty equivalent of their income as co-op members exceeds the wage $\underline{w}(\sigma^*)$ that they currently receive given by equation (5). I assume the disturbances in the income stream of the co-op are such that (as in the previous chapter) I can represent the utility function of the risk-averse members simply as $u = u(\omega,\sigma)$, where expected income ω is a "good" and risk exposure measured by σ is a "bad." The members then maximize this utility function subject to the expected income of the members being not larger than allows the cost of the loan to be repaid. (To insure that the loan is repaid with certainty, I must assume either that in those presumably rare cases where their realized residual claim is negative [i.e. realized gross income = $y^r < k(1 + \rho\mu)/(1 - t)$] co-op members have consumption-smoothing opportunities, or that these cases are sufficiently unlikely that they may be ignored.) The solution of this maximization problem determines the co-op members' expected income, just as in equation 5, except that here we have expected income depending on the members' risk choice, $y(\sigma^-)$:

$$(8)\quad \underline{\omega}(\sigma^-) = \frac{(1-m^-)[y(\sigma^-)-k(1+\rho\mu)]}{1-t}$$

This is just the labor demand equilibrium condition for an economy of worker co-ops that insures that the capital stock of the nation is stationary.

The co-op members' choice of σ will equate the marginal rate of transformation of risk into expected income to the

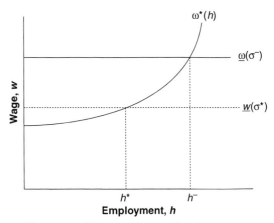

Figure 3.4 *Co-operative production may expand equilibrium employment and certainty equivalents.* If employee ownership of firms raises productivity (by improving the labor discipline environment) it may permit a higher certainty equivalent income for workers without inducing capital flight, namely, $\omega^*(\sigma^-) > \underline{w}(\sigma^*)$, even though employees' risk aversion induces them to adopt less risky and lower expected return projects. If so, then the level of employment will also increase from h^* to h^-.

marginal rate of substitution between risk and expected income as shown in Figure 2.6. The members' choice of σ^- determines the utility level to the members $u(\omega(\sigma^-), \sigma^-)$ and its certainty equivalent income $\underline{\omega}(\sigma^-)$. Suppose that $\underline{\omega}(\sigma^-) > \underline{w}(\sigma^*)$, so that members' certainty equivalent income would be raised by the formation of co-ops, then co-ops would proliferate and wage employment would be eliminated.

We can determine the level of co-op employment just as in the case of the capitalist economy, now using equation (2′) and the certainty-equivalent income implied by the solution to the utility maximization constrained by equation (8). This is depicted in Figure 3.4, which shows that the level of joblessness would fall as a result, though no more than h^- producers can belong to co-op work teams, as the $1 - h^-$ jobless are required to sustain the no-shirking condition at the certainty-equivalent income consistent with the stationarity of the country's capital stock. If, by contrast, $\omega(\sigma^-) < \underline{w}(\sigma^*)$ producers would not accept the government loans, and co-ops would not form.

But if the co-op is advantageous to the producers, why was the government's intervention required for their formation? The obvious answer – that the asset-less producers were precluded from borrowing at economically viable rates of interest – raises a more difficult question. If, as this answer implies, the asset-poor producers' subjective cost of postponing current consumption exceeds $\rho\mu$, why would they not prefer to use the government loan for consumption purposes? They would, so a successful loan program would have to embody an enforceable provision restricting the use of the corn to planting rather than eating. (The problem would in a world of inedible capital goods be simpler to address!)

Policies

Of course, actual governments and trade unions may fail to implement efficient redistributions for a variety of well-known reasons. But on the basis of the above reasoning, there appears to be ample scope for the implementation of policies capable of raising wages, employment levels, and living standards of the less well-off owners of globally immobile factors of production, even in the empirically unlikely world of hyper-globalization posited in the model. It seems likely that substantial majorities of the relevant populations would benefit from these policies, so the policies might be sustainable in democratic polities.

The model presented here and the empirical evidence suggest three ways that egalitarian redistribution in open economy settings mentioned at the outset may have succeeded. The first is by increasing productivity (or certainty-equivalent income, where risk-bearing is involved). Examples include the East Asian land redistributions and the Nordic (especially Swedish) and Singaporean policy of eliminating wage disparities among similar workers, thus putting competitive pressure on low-productivity firms and sectors and driving resources into higher-productivity uses. The second is improving the labor discipline environment, thereby reducing monitoring costs and shifting the equilibrium labor supply condition to the right. Examples include the fact that wage increases may reduce the disutility of effort (through the fair-wage effect), allow for trade union and work team participation in monitoring, and flatten the labor supply function through centralized wage bargaining. The fact that supervisory labor input is strikingly lower in countries with more egalitarian earnings distributions (Sweden, Japan) may reflect these and related effects (Gordon 1994).

The third approach is simply to redistribute labor income in a more egalitarian manner without eroding effort incentives. One way to do this, not yet implemented anywhere at the national level, is the unconditional basic income grant proposal of Philippe van Parijs and Robert van der Veen. In one respect this is equivalent to the transfer of a risk-free asset, as it unconditionally guarantees the citizen an annual flow of income in perpetuity. But unlike the wealth distribution discussed in the previous chapter, the guarantee of this flow of income typically cannot be used as collateral or equity.

There are many variants of this, starting with van Parijs and van der Veen (1986). Here is my version of how it might work. It would be designed to pay for itself without reducing the expected rate of return on capital so as to be viable even in the hyper-globalized world studied here. Instead of providing income conditional on unemployment, the government gives all adult members of the population an unconditional grant β and finances the grant by a tax on wages supplemented by the general revenue savings occasioned by setting $b = 0$. Assume the government sought to do this while maintaining the status quo work incentive situation, as modeled in Bowles (1992). As $b = 0$, the equilibrium labor supply condition (no-shirking condition) is now:

$$(2'') \quad w^* = \frac{a}{\tau(1 - h)} + b$$

As a result, the pre-existing wage rate w^*, given by (2), exceeds that required to induce workers to shirk by the amount b. So a flat tax on wage income in the amount b would restore the status quo. So the tax on wages could be the same as the erstwhile unemployment benefit. As the labor demand equation ([5] or [8]) has not been altered, the employment and (before-tax) wage level would thus remain at the status quo levels. The unconditional grant would be financed from tax revenues of hb plus savings on the elimination of the previous transfers of $(1-h)b$. All adults would thus receive an unconditional grant of $\beta = bs$, where s is the ratio of labor supply to the number of adults. The effect would be a redistribution from the employed and the unemployed to those not in the labor force, obviously favoring the old, the young, women, and other groups sometimes called "excluded."

It might be thought that the effects of the unconditional grant would be slight because family structure and other sharing arrangements allow income-pooling. But even in the empirically implausible case that all of the differentially affected groups were paired in pooling arrangements so that the expected income of each was unaffected by this policy, dispersion of unconditional income claims to those not in the labor force would predictably alter the intra-family bargaining power and possibly also the credit-market status of the previously relatively poor and powerless. This appears to be the case for the quite generous transfers to the elderly in South Africa (Ardington and Lund 1995). Of course, the grant β need not take the form of a cash transfer, but could rather be dedicated claims on health, education, recreation, and other services.

As the basic income grant example suggests, in the design and implementation of policies consistent with the supply-side egalitarian approach surveyed here, the heuristic distinction between the asset redistribution approach of the previous section and the wage and employment policies described in an earlier section will lose some of its salience. Where labor contracts embody both job security and group- or firm-level gain-sharing, for example, employees may become de facto residual claimants on a substantial fraction of the income streams they generate. Trade union bargaining can thereby capture some of the peer monitoring advantages of outright asset distribution to co-ops. This is particularly likely to be the case where the monitoring of labor effort by outsiders is ineffective (as in many information-based and other service activities), where firm-specific human resource investments are important, and where the capital required is either limited in amount or general (rather than transaction-specific, for example multiple-use equipment like computers as opposed to machinery tailored to produce a particular product), and not subject to depreciation through misuse.

The land tenure reform in West Bengal mentioned at the outset embodied exactly this logic: The outright transfer of assets to farmers was precluded by the property clauses in the Indian constitution. Rather, the farmer's share of the crop was increased from a customary one-half to three-quarters, and tenants were given protection from eviction as long as they granted the landlord the stipulated reduced share. The result was a substantial increase in the de facto rights of residual claimancy due not only to the increased share, but also to the reduced threat of eviction and hence the greater likelihood that the farmer would enjoy the future returns to land improvements and other investments.

Conclusion

Does globalization impede egalitarian redistribution? What globalization does is to make it quite costly and possibly politically unfeasible to depress (more than temporarily) the expected after-tax rate of return to capital, or to alter the relative prices of tradeable goods and services. But while globalization – at least in the *hyper* form illustrated here – fixes the relative prices of some productive services, it precludes neither an egalitarian redistribution of the tangible and human assets from which those services flow, nor the enhancement of the assets currently owned by the less well-off, nor the improvement of the institutionally determined flow of services from labor assets. Thus, gain-seeking competition does restrict the range of economically and politically sustainable relative prices, but it does not preclude egalitarian redistribution. The fundamental theorem of welfare economics defines conditions under which *any* technically feasible and Pareto-optimal distribution of welfare can be attained by *some* redistribution of assets followed by perfectly competitive exchange. The theorem is not intended as a guide to policy, but it does underline an important truth: To the extent that globalization heightens competitive pressures, it may reduce the attractiveness of redistributive approaches which rely on altering relative prices, but this hardly exhausts the set of egalitarian strategies.

An implication of the above is that the traditional vehicles of egalitarian aspirations – trade unions and states – have a different, but no less important, role to play in a highly competitive world from that they play in closed economies. The scope for conventional governmental and trade union measures that reduce the after-tax expected rate of profit below profit rates in other parts of the world is indeed restricted. But policies to implement Pareto-improving productivity gains may in some respects require a greater, rather than lesser, degree of collective interventions. Examples include an expanded role for publicly provided insurance, to address sub-optimal risk-taking due to more extensive residual claimancy and control of assets by the non-wealthy, and greater involvement of collective bargaining in more closely aligning the incentives of employers and employees with respect to both working and learning on the job.

A notable effect of globalization, unremarked upon thus far, is that (in the extreme form assumed here) it makes the non-wealthy members of a national population residual claimants on the results of both their productive efforts and their success in attenuating productivity-dampening co-ordination failures. While in competitive equilibrium the wealthy cannot get *less* than ρ, they also cannot get *more*, so productivity improvements are fully captured by the non-wealthy. It thus inverts the more common relationship in which the wealthy are the residual claimants on the income streams generated by the efforts of the less well-off. Return to Figure 3.4 and ask how were the benefits of co-op production distributed in the economy, where these proved to be viable? Some unemployed workers got jobs; employed workers raised their certainty-equivalent income. And what did the owners of capital get? Nothing; their rate of return was unchanged.

To the extent that conditions approximate those assumed in this model, then, globalization may reduce the collective-action problems confronting would-be coalitions of the non-wealthy seeking to enhance productivity by attenuating co-ordination failures. The argument is not that the non-wealthy have identical interests, but simply that the difficulty of securing mutually beneficial co-operative solutions with mobile wealth owners may be circumvented.

The theoretical results presented here suggest that efforts to raise the living standards of the less well-off may succeed where they attenuate the incentive problems arising when property rights are ill-defined or insecure, contracts are incomplete, and wealth is highly concentrated. The rationale for the egalitarian supply-side interventions summarized here – in contrast to policies restricted to pie-dividing or demand expansion – is dramatized by globalization, but it is no less compelling for closed economies.

This is not to say that globalization makes no difference. Even in the very long-run perspective taken here, the effect of globalization on the out-of-equilibrium dynamics may be decisive. A one-time aggregate demand expansion may be crucial, for example, in permanently displacing an economy from a low-road to a high-road equilibrium of the type illustrated in Figure 3.2, but the effectiveness of the necessary macroeconomic policies may be reduced by greater openness.

As we will see in the next chapter, globalization matters in another way, one that is more cultural than economic; and it will transform the politics of redistribution.

4

Globalization, cultural standardization, and the politics of social insurance

Benjamin Disraeli's "two nations ... between whom there was no intercourse and no sympathy" were the rich and the poor. It was 1845, the same year that Frederick Engels wrote the explosive *The Condition of the Working Class in England*. Since then in the advanced economies, a combination of nationalism, representative democracy, and the resulting policies of universal public education and egalitarian redistribution have bridged the cultural and economic gap considerably. The rich and the poor are still with us of course, and on a global scale the economic gap between them is far greater than when Disraeli wrote (Bourguignon and Morrison 2002). But in the richer economies the nations of Disraeli's world (and Engels') have been left behind.

Globalization, Ugo Pagano and I maintain, is an extension of nationalism, not its antithesis: it promotes cultural standardization and economic integration across national boundaries. But unlike nationalism, which in many countries had a democratic twin, globalization standardizes and integrates without providing either the international cultural solidarity or governmental institutions capable of supporting egalitarian redistribution and insurance on a global scale, while weakening some of the nation-based

This chapter is based in part on joint work with Ugo Pagano (Bowles and Pagano, 2006).

institutions for the same. In this respect a globalized world may re-create the social structure of the archetypal ancient agrarian empire: a dominant class of cosmopolitans speaking a common language (once French in many parts of Europe, Persian in Mughal India, Ottoman Turkish in the Ottoman empire, today English everywhere) and presiding over a heterogeneous and provincial underclass speaking a Babel of dialects, with little solidarity across the language groups, and weak nationally based instruments of social insurance and egalitarian redistribution.

The politics of social insurance may thus increasingly pit the cosmopolitans against the provincials (not just capital against labor, or even the high earners against the low earners, as many of the cosmopolitans are far from rich). The divide is not just linguistic. The skills of the cosmopolitans fetch a good price in a wide array of markets: They can program computers, communicate electronically, do some math, and, of course, speak English. The provincials' skills are specific to particular jobs and industries. The big difference between these two nations is not income, but rather vulnerability to economic change.

The result need not be institutional convergence to a world of uniformly minimalist welfare states, however, for the process of specialization induced by greater integration may support distinct institutional arrangements appropriate to each economy's divergent product mixes. Countries specializing in goods characterized by volatile demand or requiring high levels of specific skills will expose their citizens to increased economic risk and may be induced by globalization to strengthen their systems of social protection.

It is likely, however, that in many countries the reverse will occur. In these economies, social insurance will be compromised, leaving the provincials increasingly vulnerable to industry- or occupation-specific shocks. Where this occurs, risk reduction may take the form of forgoing specialization in occupation- or industry-specific skills, and pressures to maintain a relatively unspecialized national "portfolio" of sectors and occupations to which one may move if one's own source of livelihood is threatened.

In this case, optimal integration into the global order requires a nation to balance the marginal gains in expected income associated with greater specialization (the gains from trade) against the marginal losses associated with the enhanced risks occasioned by specialization. Individuals, likewise, will balance the benefits of specialization and diversification. The optimum for the nation will not be achieved by private decision-making, however, because the availability of a diverse portfolio of sectors and occupations is a public good. In the absence of a deliberate public policy, nations will become too specialized, and in response individuals, as a risk-reduction strategy, will forgo investments in specific skills.

I advance this thesis not as the confirmed result of a coherent model that has been adequately tested, but rather as a research agenda that is not inconsistent with what is known, and worth pursuing in light of the importance of the issues it addresses.

Globalization: the highest stage of nationalism?

Globalization is typically represented by economists as the process of integration of national economies brought about by the reduction in costs of transportation and communication and the removal of impediments to the movement of goods, people, and finance across national borders. But the same processes that have fostered the freer movement of goods, people, and finance are also creating a global culture – that is, a common language and system of meanings – among people in many nations.

Ernest Gellner (1983) defined nationalism as a movement seeking congruence between the ethnic community and the political community: "one national state, one national culture!" has been its political motto. Because I am going to claim that globalism is an extension of Gellner's nationalism, I will consider his interpretation in some detail:

> nationalism is a theory of political legitimacy which requires that
> ethnic boundaries should not cut across political ones and in
> particular that ethnic boundaries within a given state ... should
> not separate the power holders from the rest. (Gellner 1983:1)

The standardization of language and culture within a nation
is what made nationalism so radical during its early years,
especially by comparison with the structure of the agrarian
empires and other agrarian societies that it replaced.

The technological stagnation of agrarian society allowed the
endless repetition of the same production process; individuals
could perform the same jobs based on the same skills from one
generation to the next. Cultural diversity among all except the
elite stabilized these roles. It limited both horizontal and vertical mobility, and allowed the reproduction of the social
fabric over time. Cultural diversity – both between the elite
and the rest, and among the rest – was both a condition for and
a result of societal inertia. It supported the stagnation of society by depriving most of its members of the incentives to seek
social mobility. At the same time, cultural diversity along both
its horizontal and vertical dimensions was favored by the
unchanging structure of society.

The rudimentary and geographically confined division of
labor in these societies was such that ordinary farmers and
craftsmen in one locality had little need to communicate with
their counterparts in other localities. Other than the payment
of taxes or the transfer of a share of their crops to the landed,
they had even less need to interact with members of the elite.

But the broadening scope of goods markets and eventually
the emergence of labor markets and other capitalist economic
institutions radically altered the cultural requirements of
economic life. Again, Gellner:

> For the first time in human history, explicit and reasonably pre-
> cise communication becomes generally, pervasively used and
> important. In the closed local communities of the agrarian or

tribal worlds, when it came to communication, context tone, gesture, personality and situation were everything. (33)

Communication "by means of written, impersonal, context-free to-whom-it-may-concern type messages" required what Gellner termed "exo-education," that is, childhood socialization by specialists who are not members of one's family or group of close associates. Paradoxically, he wrote, "industrial society may . . . be the most highly specialized society ever: but its educational system is unquestionably the least specialized, the most universally standardized, that has ever existed" (27).

This was the process that, in Eugen Weber's phrase, turned *Peasants into Frenchmen* (Weber 1976) and villagers into citizens around the world, wherever nationalism took hold. In many cases, far from being the expression of a unified culture, states preceded the emergence of a nation. Massimo D'Azeglio (1867) had served as prime minister of Piedmont; writing about his country's unification, he observed "Italy has been made Italy, but not the Italians."

The absorption of local agrarian idioms and symbols into a standardized national culture would have been resisted more forcefully had it not provided important benefits for those making the transformation. Though Gellner did not stress this, exo-education in a common language and culture is a form of risk reduction, for it gives the exo-educated individual general skills that may be deployed in a variety of pursuits, rather than the occupation- or sector-specific skills that were passed on by parents engaged in the forms of endo-education typical of agrarian societies.

To see this, suppose that uncertainty takes the form of the occurrence of either a status quo state, in which the individual continues his current livelihood with income y, or a bad state, in which there is no demand for the individual's particular line of work, and he thus must pursue some other livelihood in which he receives $y(1 - s)$ where s is a measure of the degree to which his skills are specific to the initial livelihood. Suppose the status quo occurs with probability $p > ½$. The individual's expected income is:

(1) $E(y) = py + (1 - p)y(1 - s)$

and the variance of his realized income is $p(1 - p)(ys)^2$.

The structural and technical dynamism of capitalism arguably lowered the probability of the status quo persisting, increasing the chance of an unpleasant surprise. But exo-education also lowered s, the specificity of a worker's skill set. Because of cultural homogenization coupled with the spread of mass exo-education, investments in human capital became more general and (in bad states) more easily deployed in alternative uses. In the process of creative destruction, successful creation was now greatly remunerated while, at the same time, the costs of destruction and failure were substantially decreased by the increased reversibility and liquidity of human skills.

If, as Gellner says, the emergence of mobility and markets required some minimum degree of cultural homogenization, their development also implied a dramatic further increase in cultural homogenization that, in most cases, caused a deepening of the feelings of national solidarity. Cultural homogenization and solidarity within large, well-defined territories are, thus, two complementary aspects of nationalism. At the same time, they are also substitutes, in the sense that they can act as alternative insurance devices against the risk associated with the specialization of skills in a volatile market society (D'Antoni and Pagano 2002).

While the nation state originated this self-reinforcing process, it could hardly be contained forever within the boundaries of nation states. Some nation states developed a sense of a "global mission" and started doing to other languages and traditions what the nation state had done to the diverse cultures and dialects within its boundaries. Included are Britain with its Commonwealth, the Russian Empire in its last manifestation as the Soviet Union, and the US with its federal system, its frontier, its ethnic melting-pot, and its global ambitions.

In many cases, nation states – especially the non-English-speaking ones – now find themselves in opposition to the further advancement of the very process of cultural homogenization that a century earlier had been their main task and, perhaps, the fundamental reason for their existence. The former cultural standardizers of the Age of Nationalism have become the victims of standardization on an even grander scale, a historical nemesis that threatens the survival of their own traditions. The energetic defense of the French language – once the lingua franca of elites as far east as St. Petersburg – and the ongoing battles within the World Trade Organization about national subsidization of cultural production reflect this development.

Cosmopolitans and provincials

But the emerging global world order marks a new age, as different from the nationalisms with which it now contends as it is from the ancient empires with which it is inevitably compared.

It is different from the empires that had in the past politically unified large areas of Europe, Northern India, and China. The Roman Empire of antiquity and, after that, the Holy Roman Empire never posed a comparable challenge to cultural diversity. The universal culture and the lingua franca remained the distinctive mark of the ruling classes. The same could be said with only slightly less force of the Mughal and Ottoman empires. In the ancient empires, a modicum of political unity was accomplished in the absence of cultural unity. Globalization appears likely to do the opposite.

Modern globalization spreads global culture well beyond a ruling minority. But while the economic integration and cultural standardization accomplished by globalization may favor greater political integration, the very modest degree of global political unity today is mainly based on the dominance of the US, on local processes of political integration such as the European Community, and on the limited governance of some international institutions.

In addition to its lack of well-defined boundaries, the nature of modern globalism is also fundamentally different from nationalism. The political unity of the nation state made possible a distinctive method of risk reduction: cultural homogenization and social protection combined to reduce the risks associated with the market economy. Tax and transfer policies that redistributed income from the lucky to the unlucky decreased the costs of risk exposure, while those workers who had acquired job-specific skills were buffered from the vagaries of the labor market by employment safeguards and unemployment insurance. The willingness of the lucky to pay to insure the unlucky even after the dice had been rolled was enhanced by the feeling that "it could have been me," itself a product of cultural homogenization.

Modern globalism not only lacks the international institutions allowing social protection on a world scale, it also makes the traditional forms of social protection offered by the nation state increasingly problematic. As we saw in the previous chapter, increased mobility of capital and other factors of production owned by the relatively well-off have provided a rationale for shifting taxation away from these factors, thus raising the cost of policies designed to redistribute income within the nation state. More competitive goods markets, along with greater mobility of capital and professional labor, have also reduced the scope for trade union bargaining (Choi 2004) and, in some countries, weakened job protection.

Moreover, cultural standardization – the other instrument by which national economies have traditionally insured their citizens against the risks of market mobility – is very limited in the internationally integrated economy. Access to the dominant cultural standard – English fluency – is much more

unequally distributed on a world scale than the national equivalents within national boundaries – fluency in the national
language. The result is a division between those who have
inherited or acquired mobile intellectual assets that are easily
redeployed throughout the global economy – the *cosmopolitans* – and those that have skills that are less mobile and more
specific to the national economy – the *provincials*. The distinction, roughly, is that between the skills typical of people working in Silicon Valley and Detroit, or between Bangalore and
Kanpur.

Cosmopolitans – even those with modest incomes – may
prefer to replace social protection with cultural standardization as their preferred form of insurance, withdrawing
where possible from the mutual insurance system that
characterizes nation states. Like financial capital, these
workers may become difficult to tax. Their relatively easy
exit from a national system of mutual insurance makes it
even more difficult to finance the traditional forms of social
protection supplied by the nation state and worsens the
situation of those workers who lack access to the global
cultural standard.

The partial cultural standardization associated with modern
globalism may thus create a worldwide cosmopolitan elite
communicating among themselves in a new Latin that cannot
be used as a working language by the vast majority of the
populations among whom they live. The result would be an
information-age equivalent to the old agrarian societies
studied by Gellner, presided over by an elite whose high
culture unites them around the globe as it separates them
from the rest of their own societies, which are in turn separated
one from another by the persistence of linguistic and cultural
divisions. The fact that many workers of modest incomes will
count themselves among the cosmopolitans differentiates
modern globalism from the ancient agrarian societies and
empires. But, as we will see, this may also exacerbate the
challenge facing the nationally based welfare state.

The politics of insurance

To show this, I will model the social insurance preferences of a citizenry of risk-averse individuals. I am here following the work of Sinn (1995) and Domar and Musgrave (1944), who modeled the welfare state as a process of redistribution from the lucky to the unlucky, rather than from the rich to the poor. My model is based on the ideas in D'Antoni and Pagano (2002). Preferences among citizens are identical and are entirely self-regarding, but due to differences in the nature of their income-earning assets, they differ in expected income and risk exposure. Like those in the credit market model of Chapter 2, the richer citizens are less risk-averse than the poor, that is, citizens are decreasingly risk-averse.

Suppose the income y of an individual with a given set of assets varies in response to stochastic shocks according to:

$$(2) \quad y = z\sigma + g$$

where g is expected income and z is a random variable with mean zero and unit standard deviation. Thus, σ is the standard deviation of income, a measure of risk. Then we write the individual's utility function as:

$$(3) \quad v = v(g, \sigma)$$

With suitable restrictions on its partial derivatives, this function expresses the individual's positive valuation of higher levels of expected income (expected income is a good: $v_g > 0$) and negative valuation of more uncertain income (risk is a "bad": $v_\sigma < 0$).

The indifference loci representing an individual with decreasing risk aversion appear in Figure 4.1. Recall (from Chapter 2) that they are increasing and convex in σ, flat at the vertical intercept ($v_\sigma = 0$ for $\sigma = 0$), become flatter for increasing g when $\sigma > 0$, and become steeper for increasing σ, and that the

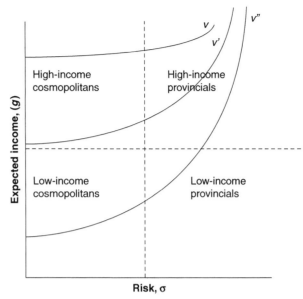

Figure 4.1 *Indifference loci of a decreasingly risk-averse citizenry with a taxonomy of citizens according to their assets and associated expected income and risk exposure.* Provincials are more risk-exposed and hence more risk-averse than cosmopolitans with similar income because their assets are specific to particular occupations and industries.

slope of an indifference locus, $(-v_\sigma/v_g) \equiv \eta(g,\sigma)$, is the marginal rate of substitution between risk and expected income. Thus, $\eta(g,\sigma)$ is a measure of the level of risk aversion experienced by an individual faced with a given level of expected income (g) and risk (σ). It is clear that this measure of risk aversion is increasing in the level of risk exposure (movements to the right in Figure 4.1) and decreasing in the level of expected income (movements upwards in Figure 4.1). Figure 4.1 also indicates the (σ,g) pairs associated with four classes of citizens demarcated by their income levels and risk exposure.

Now suppose the citizens "buy" some risk reduction at the cost of a reduced expected income. They do this by collectively agreeing to tax themselves at a rate t, paying to each citizen an equal share of the proceeds of the tax, $ty^o(1-w)$, where y^o is mean income and w (think "waste") is the proportional loss in distributed benefits due to administration, deadweight losses, capital flight, or other costs of operating the system. The citizen's post-tax and transfer-expected income is now:

(4) $g^t = g(1-t) + ty^o(1-w)$

and its standard deviation is $\sigma(1-t)$.

The tax is a form of insurance because it reduces not only expected income, but also the standard deviation of income. The effect on expected income (differentiating [4] with respect to t) is $-(g - y^o(1-w))$, and the effect of variations in t on the standard deviation of income is $-\sigma$. Thus, for $\sigma > 0$ this "insurance technology" implies a "price of insurance," ρ. We can express this as a cost–benefit ratio, namely the ratio of the marginal loss in expected income associated with an increase in the tax (the cost: $g - y^o(1 - w)$) to the marginal reduction in risk exposure associated with an increase in the tax (the benefit, which is just σ itself). This ratio of the two effects of varying t may be termed the marginal rate of transformation of expected income into risk reduction:

(5) $\rho = (g - y^o(1-w))/\sigma$

If she could unilaterally determine the tax rate, the citizen whose expected income is less than $y^o(1 - w)$ could "purchase" insurance at negative cost (i.e. $\rho < 0$), benefitting from both the risk reduction and the fact that her transfer will exceed her tax payment. Equation (5) shows that the price of insurance is increasing in expected income and declining in risk exposure, as one would expect.

What tax and transfer level would citizens prefer, if they were in a position to determine t? A citizen with $g > y^o(1 - w)$ would maximize her expected after-tax-and-transfer utility, namely $v^t = v(g^t(t), \sigma^t(t))$, by selecting the value of t that equates the

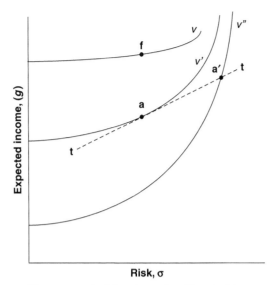

Figure 4.2 *A citizen's optimal level of insurance*
The person with assets which the absence of insurance would
yield the outcome at *a'* prefers to purchase insurance at the price
indicated by the slope of the "insurance technology" locus **tt**, as a
result attaining point **a** and increasing her utility from *v''* to *v'*.

price of insurance (the marginal rate of transformation of
expected income into risk reduction) to the marginal rate of
substitution between risk and expected income, i.e. $\rho = \eta$. In
Figure 4.2 this optimum is point **a** for a person whose assets
placed her at **a'**.

A person whose assets placed him at point **f**, better off than
at point **a'** and no more risk-exposed, would prefer a tax rate
of zero. (If he could, he would happily run the tax system in
reverse, setting $t<0$, and with all citizens paying a given lump
sum in return for a linear subsidy of his earnings, but I will
not consider this case.) Thus, it seems we can divide the
citizenry into two classes: those whose asset position yields
a positive optimal tax rate, and those who would prefer no
social insurance. Here is how that is done.

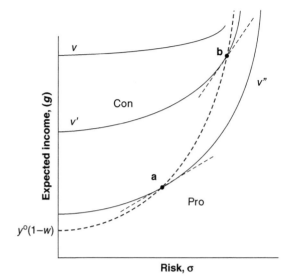

Figure 4.3 *Social insurance and the zero-tax locus*
Shown are the citizen's indifference loci and two light dashed
lines indicating the available insurance technology with slopes
equal to the marginal rate of transformation of reduced expected
income into reduced risk. Where these are tangent to the
indifference locus, the citizen favors a zero tax rate. Individuals
whose assets place them at points **a** or **b** favor zero social
insurance. The *zero-tax locus* – the curved dashed line – is the
locus of all such points. Thus, those above the zero-tax locus
oppose social insurance; those below it support it.

We know that an individual with no risk exposure ($\sigma = 0$)
and $g = y^o(1 - w)$ will be indifferent to the choice of t, for it
will affect neither his risk exposure nor his expected income.
Now consider a person for whom g exceeds $y^o(1 - w)$ by a
small amount. If the person is not risk-exposed, he will
oppose social insurance; but there will be some level of risk
exposure that will make him indifferent between no tax and a
positive tax rate, namely that for which $\rho = \eta$. The (g,σ) pairs
for which $\rho = \eta$ form the zero-tax locus in Figure 4.3. Those
whose assets place them above the zero-tax locus will oppose

social insurance, while those below it will support some level of taxation. Not surprisingly the zero-tax locus is upward-sloping: Higher expected income and less risk exposure make social insurance less of a bargain.

This view of voter preferences coupled with the earlier observation that a person with job-specific skills is more risk-exposed receives support from a study by Iversen and Soskice (2001). They estimated the relationship between support for redistributive measures and the degree of specificity of an individual's skills in two social survey data sets in 11 advanced democracies in the late 1990s. Conditioned on other influences on political preferences (income, sex, employment status, party affiliation, and age) the degree of skill specificity (being located farther to the right in Figure 4.3) is a highly significant determinant of support for redistributive policies, equal in effect size to income (that is a standard deviation difference in skill specificity is associated with a difference in redistributive preferences that is equivalent in size to a standard deviation difference in income).

Globalism vs. the welfare state?

We can now consider three effects of globalism. First, the costs of redistribution may increase. In my model this is just an increase in w, which (from [5]) has the effect of raising the price of insurance, increasing the slope of the **tt** locus in Figure 4.2, and thereby shifting the zero-tax locus downwards. As a result, more citizens are included in the con rather than the pro classes. Second, if economic integration raises incomes (as one may expect it to do on average), it will move citizens upwards in Figure 4.3, leading to reduced support for the welfare state.

Third, globalism may alter the distribution of citizens in (g,σ) space. Rodrik (1998), Garrett (1998), and others have suggested that openness may increase support for the welfare state by increasing risk exposure (shifting voters to the right in Figure 4.3). These effects appear to have been at work in a number of countries, including those Nordic nations that pioneered the institutions we now call the welfare state (Moene and Wallerstein 1995a).

While I believe these effects to be operative in many cases, I have above stressed another possible shift in the distribution of citizens: the emergence of a large class of cosmopolitans, including many with middling incomes. To dramatize the importance of this shift (through a bit of exaggeration), consider a "prototype nineteenth-century economy." It is composed of what Alchian and Demsetz (1972) called "classical capitalist firms" whose single owner hires (in a daily spot market) workers with few firm-specific skills (what Marx termed abstract labor). An owner of tangible assets in such a firm is highly risk-exposed, as there is a substantial loss in the value of an asset once it is installed – in the modern economy, typically well over half of the initial cost (Asplund 2000). By contrast, the workers' job assets – abstract labor – make them much less risk-exposed. In this world, the owners would be classed among the high-income provincials in Figure 4.1, while the workers would be the low-income cosmopolitans: The distribution of citizens would lie in the "north-east" and "south-west" quadrants. Of course, most workers' expected incomes would be such that $g < y^o(1-w)$, so most workers and all but the very rich owners would support the welfare state.

This economy is imaginary, but the contrast between it and what may be the emerging global order is striking. Workers now receive substantial job rents, that is, pay above their next-best alternative. These are the result either of workers' firm-specific skills or of the widespread use by employers of contingent renewal strategies of labor discipline that result in equilibrium wages in excess of workers' reservation wages (described in Bowles, 2004). And while industrial assets are still highly specific, many of the assets used in the sales and service sectors of the economy (far larger than manufacturing in most advanced economies) are quite general (buildings and computers, for example). Moreover, in contrast to the fictive classical capitalist firm, ownership of these assets is highly diversified. Both diversification and the more general nature of these assets have the effect of greatly reducing risk exposure. Additionally, there is now a large class of salaried employees whose high level of general skills, including their access to the global cultural standard, greatly reduces their risk exposure. These are the new cosmopolitans.

Figure 4.4 illustrates these shifts. The inner dashed contour indicates a greater density of citizens, and the increasingly "north-west, south-east" array of citizens suggests a new dimension of support and opposition for social insurance, namely the degree of access to the global cultural standard.

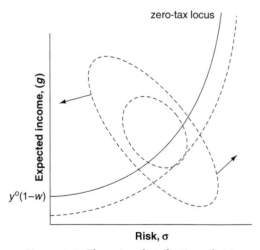

Figure 4.4 *Changing distribution of citizens and zero-tax locus under the influence of globalization*
The dashed contours give the distribution of voters. The dashed zero-tax locus shows the effect of the increased price of insurance and increased cost of redistribution, w.

One cannot rule out a "twin peaks" distribution emerging, with a concentration of well-to-do cosmopolitans and less well-off provincials divided by a ravine of cultural disparity and divergent economic opportunity. To avoid unnecessary simplification, I have deliberately not specified how the national tax rate will be selected, so one cannot predict the effect of this "twin peaks" scenario, should it evolve, on the amount of support for social insurance in general.

Globalization and institutional convergence

I said that there are three effects of globalization in this model: increased costs of insurance, higher income, and a redistribution of citizens in (g,σ) space. But there is a fourth: The process of economic integration is also one of specialization, the effect of which is that countries will become more distinct in the kinds of skills and other assets that their product mix requires. Suppose there are two goods, grain and plows, and that in the absence of international exchange each of two countries would employ equal numbers of worker-citizens producing the two goods. The demand for plows, as an investment good, is highly volatile (it is proportional to the *change in the level* of demand for grain), while the demand for grain, a consumption good, is less volatile, depending on the *level* of income and population. Because of these differences in risk exposure, within each country those employed producing plows (except for the very well-paid among them) will be supporters of insurance, while, except for the poorest, those growing grain will oppose it.

Following economic integration, however, differential comparative advantage means that one country specializes in plow production and the other in grain production. As a result, the voters in Plowland are now almost uniformly supporters of social insurance (unless the gains from trade have made them sufficiently rich), while the citizens of Grainia are equally opposed (unless, of course, openness has sufficiently increased risk exposure in Grainia to offset the reduction in risk associated with specialization in the less volatile good). The result is that economic integration may lead to greater institutional diversity rather than, as is sometimes predicted, and as Keynes feared, institutional homogenization.

Only slightly less transparent is the case where sectors differ in the importance of specific skills, and integration leads to some countries specializing in producing general-skill goods and others in specific-skill goods. This view is advanced by Hall and Soskice (2001:38): "national institutional frameworks provide nations with comparative advantage. In the presence of trade, these advantages should give rise to ... specialization." In turn, according to Hall and Soskice, specialization in those goods for which a country has a comparative advantage is likely to support institutional divergence.

In these cases, the specialization associated with integration may enhance the diversity of "technology-institutional equilibria" (Pagano 1993). Hall and Soskice have interpreted the differing social policies of the US and Germany in this light, the German product mix requiring high levels of specific skills, the protection of which through generous unemployment benefits and other forms of job protection is supported by large majorities of the electorate. The presence of these social protection policies in turn allows these specific skill-intensive industries to attract labor and remain viable in international competition.

The presumption that globalism induces institutional convergence is based on a simple, but wrong model in which global competition is represented as a kind of selection pressure operating to force the elimination of inferior designs. But geography and history combine to make specialization advantageous, and given that some institutions are better able to co-ordinate the production of some goods, while other institutions do better for other goods, the increase in selection pressure may produce divergence rather than convergence (Pagano 2001).

With Marianna Belloc I have extended this reasoning by noting that pre-existing cultural and institutional differences may be a source of differential comparative advantage and specialization even among countries that are identical with respect to factor endowments (geography) and technology (Belloc and Bowles 2012). Where both cultures (the distribution of preferences in the population) and institutions (the distribution of distinct types of contract) co-evolve endogenously by a decentralized process of individual updating we show that multiple cultural-institutional equilibria exist and that even if one of these is strictly inferior to the other (a move to the other would benefit both workers and employers), trade liberalization does not induce convergence. In fact, trade between the two economies makes convergence less likely because it allows the country at the inferior cultural-institutional equilibrium to specialize in the product that it is "least bad" at producing.

This model, along with Pagano's technology-institutional equilibrium model, resonates with historical data. It was economic integration – not autarky – that induced the divergence in institutional structure between the sugar-growing islands of the Caribbean on the one hand and those economies of Central America, such as Costa Rica, whose geography is ill-suited to plantation crops. Another example is the importance of family-owned firms in the Italian economy, which distinguishes it from most of its competitors, and is explained by the fact that, due to economic integration, Italy increasingly specializes in those goods for which this form of governance is effective. And we have already seen that it was the very openness of the small Nordic nations that pushed them to diverge from the institutional structures of capitalist nations and to develop their particular brand of welfare state after the Second World War.

John Maynard Keynes (in the quotation opening the previous chapter) warned that a global *laissez-faire* regime would place nations in a straitjacket of policy convergence.

And to the extent that some policies of social insurance are simply inferior designs, while other nations' lack of social insurance are also simply flawed designs, globalism will increase the pressures for policy convergence. But one cannot say if these forces will be offset by the persistence and even divergence of distinct institutional arrangements associated with high levels of specialization.

Optimal specialization?

Investment in general rather than industry- or occupation-specific skills and assets is a means of reducing risk exposure, and thus may be a substitute for the kinds of social insurance modeled above. What could be termed a cosmopolitan risk-reduction strategy may become increasingly attractive in those countries in which economic integration creates pressures to reduce the scope of social insurance and job protection. But, unless emigration is a feasible option, even those with general assets are vulnerable in an economy specialized in the production of a limited range of goods. This is because the protection against adverse price shocks offered by general assets takes the form of an ability to redeploy these skills in other industries or occupations for which the relevant prices are substantially uncorrelated. The shock-induced relocation of inputs from one industry to another will generate adverse price effects, even when the assets being relocated are entirely general. But in an economy with a diverse "portfolio" of industries and occupations, these effects will be small as long as the adversely affected sectors are small relative to the size of the economy as a whole.

The existence of such a diverse "portfolio" of industries and occupations is, however, a public good in the sense that it provides general risk-reduction benefits that are not accounted for in the individual's utility- or profit-maximizing choices concerning occupational or sectoral location. For this reason economies guided entirely by private incentives will tend to overspecialize. And in response to the associated risk exposure, individuals will resist investing in job-specific skills, effectively over-generalizing their human portfolio compared with what would have been utility-maximizing in the absence of economy-wide over-specialization. Global economic integration will exacerbate this market failure *if* it increases risk exposure and reduces the scope of substitute forms of risk reduction such as social insurance.

Cultural diversity and egalitarian redistribution

Similar reasoning can be extended beyond the specificity of job skills to study linguistic and ethnic diversity, aspects of a nation's culture usually thought to undermine support for redistributive policies. Massimo D'Antoni and Ugo Pagano advanced the idea that, like job-specific skills, cultural diversity within a nation inhibits geographical, occupational, and other forms of mobility when economic adversity requires a job change or relocation, thereby exposing citizens to greater economic risks and inducing them to demand more adequate levels of economic insurance from the state (D'Antoni and Pagano 2002). The idea is simple. Consider an individual with a given set of skills and no other sources of income. Suppose the individual speaks a language shared by relatively few individuals and is considering learning some commonly spoken language. Think of a Danish worker contemplating taking English or German courses. Learning a lingua franca is costly, but, by providing access to otherwise inaccessible labor markets in which one's skills may be in demand, it reduces the expected cost of losing one's job (supposing that job loss is the risk to which the citizen is exposed).

We can compare learning the lingua franca to an alternative insurance mechanism, namely a policy of redistribution, taking the basic income grant introduced in the last chapter as an example. The basic income grant (BIG) provides a fixed income (the grant) at the cost of paying taxes that are levied on a risk-exposed income stream. Thus, it substitutes a fixed transfer for a variable flow of income. Because the degree of risk aversion varies with the level of risk exposure and the BIG limits risk exposure, the provision of a BIG reduces the citizen's risk aversion and hence limits her demand for the implicit insurance provided by a lingua franca. For analogous reasons it is also true that policies promoting learning the lingua franca (requiring that it be taught in school, for example) will reduce the demand for social insurance. Not surprisingly, then, the BIG and the lingua franca are what economists call substitutes – more of one reduces the value of the other. Or to put it more positively, linguistic diversity and economic security are complements: Each enhances the citizens' benefits of having more of the other.

Suppose the individual has two choices. Unlike the citizens considered thus far (who were simply assumed to have a skill set that was more or less job-specific), she may select a degree of specialization in her training. For example, she might study a specific physical therapy technique, for example, rather than liberal arts; the latter would give her a lower expected income (net of the costs of education), but greater occupational flexibility and hence less risk exposure. Her second choice is how much to invest in learning the lingua franca.

Suppose (as in Chapter 2) that in the absence of the BIG and any investment in the lingua franca, an individual's realized income, y, is her expected income g plus deviations from expected income that cannot be predicted in advance where σ is the standard deviation of income, a measure of risk. States among which the individual must choose differ in the degree of risk to which the individual is exposed, σ.

The risk-reduction effects of the BIG are readily studied in this framework, as they result in a leftward shift in the risk-return function due to the fact that the basic income is not risk-exposed, and it is funded by taxes that reduce the

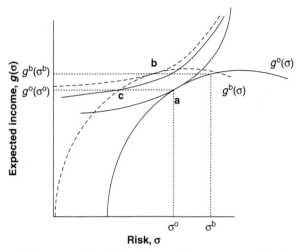

Figure 4.5 *The BIG reduces risk exposure and induces greater risk-taking, resulting in an increase in expected income*

risk-exposed income stream, thereby substituting a certain income for the tax portion of the uncertain income. In Figure 4.5 I show a horizontal displacement of the g function indicating that the BIG is a pure risk-reduction intervention without income-reducing effects that might be associated with other conditional risk-reduction policies. (I have shown in Bowles 1992 that a substantial BIG can be introduced without adversely affecting incentives to work and invest.)

In the figure, the pre- and post-BIG risk choices and expected incomes are indicated by superscripts o and b respectively and by points **a** and **b** respectively. Point **c**, resulting from an unchanged level of risk-taking after the introduction of the BIG, cannot be a utility maximum because the indifference locus at **c** must be flatter than at **a**, while the slope of the g function is unchanged (so the tangency required for a maximum must be at some higher level of risk-taking). The increase in the level of risk-taking is due to both the citizen's lesser level of risk exposure and (given that risk aversion is decreasing in expected income) her higher level of expected income at point **b**. This is just another way of affirming the main idea in Evsy Domar and Richard Musgrave's 1944 paper: Income redistribution may induce greater risk-taking by citizens (Domar and Musgrave 1944).

It is worth noting that if the BIG were a "leaky bucket," so that the taxes collected greatly exceeded the grants made due to administrative or other costs, it could reduce expected income for any given level of risk choice. This would shift the *g* function down as well as to the left). As a consequence the above result might not hold, as the reduced expected income would enhance risk aversion and could offset the effects of reduced risk exposure.

To determine the effect of learning a lingua franca (for the moment in the absence of the BIG) we imagine that one can incur costs to learn various amounts of the lingua franca, and that learning more is associated with greater risk reduction, as it makes one's skills more valuable in a wider range of alternative labor markets. Thus, we posit a cultural risk-reduction technology that for a cost of $f\lambda$ reduces risk exposure by an amount λ. (The details of the model are in the appendix to this chapter – see pp. 166–7.)

In Figure 4.6 the individual could select point **a** as before, but if it costs *f* to reduce risk exposure, then, as long as this cost is less than the degree of risk aversion (the slope of the indifference locus), the citizen would do better to learn some of the lingua franca, choosing point **a** but then trading off some expected income for reduced risk exposure. But the citizen could do even better by adopting a higher level of risk (σ^L) and learning even more of the lingua franca. This is shown in the figure by point **x** (the citizen's choice of risk and expected income) and point **L** (for Language, the citizen's experienced level of risk exposure and reduced expected

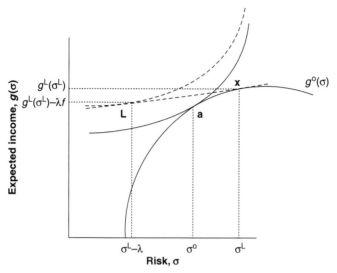

Figure 4.6 *Learning the lingua franca reduces the experienced risk level and induces a higher choice of risk*

income net of the costs of language study). Here the citizen's optimum is given by equating the marginal rate of transformation of increased risk into increased expected income (g'), with the marginal rate of transformation of reduced expected income (the language tuition) into reduced risk in the cultural insurance technology (which is just f). The expected income net of the language costs need not increase; the contrast with the BIG case arises because language training is costly (it uses up resources that have alternative productive uses) while the BIG is not (because its grants are transfers of claims on resources, not expenditures of resources).

It is now clear why the lingua franca and the BIG are substitutes: What they both accomplish – risk reduction – is subject to diminishing returns, so that more of one reduces the marginal value of the other. Would a sufficiently large BIG entirely eliminate the citizen's motivation to learn the lingua franca?

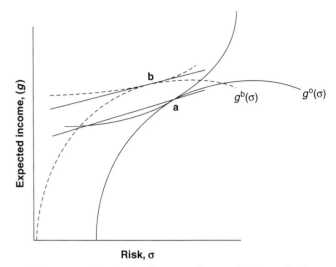

Figure 4.7 *The BIG reduces and may eliminate the incentive to learn the lingua franca*
At point **a** the upward-sloping line gives the individual's cultural risk-reduction technology (with slope *f*) and shows that acquiring the lingua franca would be optimal (as explained with respect to Figure 4.6). The reduced level of risk exposure and higher expected income of the citizen at the post-BIG outcome (point **b**) makes the citizen indifferent to learning the lingua franca.

We just saw that the individual would choose to learn the lingua franca in the absence of the BIG, and we reproduce this result at point **a** in Figure 4.7, where, because *f* is less than the degree of risk aversion, the individual could benefit by learning the lingua franca. But is this also true if the BIG is introduced? It need not be. In the figure I show the level of the BIG such that, given the resulting risk exposure of the citizen (point **b**), there would be no benefit to learning the lingua franca. A smaller BIG would reduce the optimal acquisition of the lingua franca, but not eliminate it.

Not surprisingly, the converse is also true: The availability of a cultural risk-reduction technology – learning the lingua franca in our model – that is sufficiently effective (*f* is sufficiently small) will reduce the demand for a BIG. This can be seen in Figure 4.7, where the demand for the risk reduction associated with the BIG is just the degree of risk aversion. At point **a** this is considerable, indicating that the citizen would be willing to incur a substantial expected income loss in order to reduce risk exposure. Even though acquiring some of the lingua franca induces the citizen to incur more risk, the resulting degree of risk exposure is reduced, and the citizen's willingness to pay (in expected income losses) for a reduction in risk is reduced (the slope of the indifference locus at **L** is less than at **a**).

Learning the lingua franca in this model is just a metaphor for any costly activity that reduces an individual's risk exposure by making her income-earning assets less vulnerable to culturally local shocks. Cultivating culturally diverse network ties could play a similar role. The example returns us to the many reasons (put aside at the outset), other than risk reduction, that an individual might want to invest in less culturally specific skills. It also reminds us that those who invest in either more universal skills or skills specific to some other culture provide important benefits to their fellow citizens and non-citizens alike. Thus, one cannot infer from the analysis here that we should count the reduced demand for learning the lingua franca and the possible contribution that this makes to cultural diversity as a reason to support the BIG (and similar risk-reducing public policies).

But the reasoning does provide a counter to the widespread and empirically founded concern that ethnic, linguistic, religious, and other differences among citizens might reduce support for public policies that redistribute income and economic opportunities to a society's less fortunate members. We have here an example of the opposite. It is cultural unification – learning the lingua franca – that undermines support for egalitarian redistribution; cultural diversity provides citizens with a reason to support the BIG.

Conclusion

If I am correct, understanding the impact of cultural and economic globalism on national policies for redistribution and social insurance would be advanced by greater attention to the degree of specificity of the assets held by people and to the possible emergence of a large class of cosmopolitans who have little interest in traditional social insurance policies and who feel (at best) weak solidarity with co-resident provincials. It would be valuable to know, as an empirical matter, if among people with similar incomes those with more general education tend to oppose social insurance. Equally important is the possible divergence of national institutional trajectories as a consequence of more advanced levels of specialization made possible by global integration. Are there empirical cases in which divergence in social insurance policies can be plausibly linked to divergent patterns of specialization following economic integration?

The models also suggest some interesting puzzles. Why, for example, do the children of the relatively well-off tend to be cosmopolitans, while the children of the less well-off tend to be the provincials? Given the greater risk aversion of the latter group (parents and children alike), one might have expected the reverse, namely, that the children of workers should study liberal arts, while the children of their employers could take a chance on some specific engineering degree. Of course in most countries, the education experienced by the two groups does differ, but not in this way: The children of the well-to-do typically follow a classical liberal arts education including languages, while others tend to acquire specific occupational skills. Because there is a substantial element of choice involved in implementing this difference, the puzzle remains. Are the general skills of the cosmopolitans complementary with wealth, so that the asset-poor benefit less from learning English, or programming skills, or Homer, for example, than the children of the well-to-do?

One cannot answer these questions using models – like the one presented here – in which the politics of redistribution is based on self-interested preferences among citizens differentiated only by the kinds of asset they hold. Citizens are ethical as well as self-interested, and they care about the well-being of others. Taking account of this is an essential part of the new economics of inequality and redistribution and the subject of the next chapter.

5

Reciprocity, altruism, and the politics of redistribution

The modern welfare state is a remarkable human achievement. In Europe and North America, a substantial fraction of total income is regularly transferred from the better-off to the less well-off, and the governments that preside over these transfers are regularly endorsed by publics (Atkinson 1999). The modern welfare state is thus the most significant case in human history of a voluntary egalitarian redistribution of income among total strangers. What accounts for its popular support?

A compelling case can be made that people support the welfare state because they think it is the right thing to do. It conforms to a behavioral schema which we call *strong reciprocity*. Strong reciprocity is a propensity to co-operate and share with others similarly disposed, even at personal cost, and a willingness to punish those who violate co-operative and other social norms, even when punishing is personally costly and cannot be expected to result in net personal gains in the future. Strong reciprocity goes beyond self-interested forms of co-operation, which include acting tit-for-tat and what biologists call *reciprocal altruism* (Trivers 1971), which is really just self-interest with a long time horizon. Genuine altruism, in the standard biological sense of the

This chapter is based on joint work with Christina Fong and Herbert Gintis (Fong, Bowles, and Gintis, 2005).

131

term, is what motivates actors to help others in situations where the actor would increase her payoffs by not helping (Kerr, Godfrey-Smith, and Feldman 2004).

Economists have, for the most part, deployed an empirically implausible theory of self-regarding human motivation to explain who votes for redistribution. The most widely accepted model of the demand for redistribution in economics is based on the median voter model, which holds that each voter desires a personal wealth-maximizing level of redistribution. Under appropriate assumptions, it follows that the redistribution implemented by a government elected under a majority-rule system is that which maximizes the personal wealth of the median-income voter. Because the distribution of wealth is generally skewed to the right (there are a few very rich individuals), the median voter is poorer than the mean voter and will therefore benefit from a proportional tax on wealth (or income), the proceeds of which are redistributed to all citizens in a lump-sum equal payment. Thus the median voter demands a positive level of redistribution.

An important implication of this model is that demand for redistribution is less among richer individuals (Roberts 1977). But personal income is a surprisingly poor predictor of support for redistribution (Gilens 1999, Fong 2001). A large fraction of the poor oppose income redistribution, and a large fraction of the rich support it. Among respondents of a nationally representative US survey who have annual household incomes of at least $150,000 and expect their lives to improve in the next 5 years, 24 percent respond that the government should redistribute wealth by heavy taxes on the rich, and 67 percent respond that the "government in Washington, DC should make every possible effort to improve the social and economic position of the poor" (Gallup 1998). Equally striking is the fact that among those with annual family incomes of less than $10,000 who did not expect to be better off in 5 years, 32 percent report that the government should *not* redistribute wealth by heavy taxes on the rich, and 23 percent say that "the poor should help themselves rather than having the government make every possible effort to improve the ... position of the poor."

Thus, while income does explain some individual differences in redistributive attitudes, other motives appear to be at work. Abundant evidence from across the social sciences – much of it focusing on the US, with some similar findings from other countries around the world – has shown that when people blame the poor for their poverty, they support less redistribution than when they believe that the poor are poor through no fault of their own. That is, generosity towards the poor is conditional on the belief that the poor work hard (Williamson 1974, Heclo 1986, Farkas and Robinson 1996, Gilens 1999, Miller 1999). For instance, in a 1972 sample of white women in Boston, the perceived work ethic of the poor was a far better predictor of support for aid to the poor than one's family income (Williamson 1974). Moffitt, Ribar, and Wilhelm (1998) were among the first economists to report findings on this relationship. They used the General Social Survey, a large, nationally representative data set with observations in nearly every year since 1972 to show that those who believe that people get ahead by "lucky breaks or help from others" rather than hard work prefer more spending on welfare. My co-author in this research, Christina Fong (2001), used nationally representative data from a 1998 Gallup Social Audit to show that the effects of beliefs about the causes of high or low incomes on demands for redistribution are surprisingly large and cannot be explained by missing measures of self-interest. Alesina, Glaeser, and Sacerdote (2001) have reported related findings from the World Values Survey on the attitudes of Americans and Europeans. Americans have much stronger beliefs that poverty is caused by laziness; 60 percent of Americans say the poor are lazy, compared with just 27 percent of Europeans.

My interpretation of these findings is that people are willing to help the poor, but they withdraw support when they perceive that the poor may cheat or not try hard enough to be self-sufficient and morally upstanding. Within economics, this view is most similar to the taxpayer-resentment view of the demand for redistribution modeled by Besley and Coate (1992), and the effect of reciprocity on redistributive public finance by Serge Kolm (1984).

Economists have raised convincing objections to the survey evidence that seems to show that voters' support for redistribution reflects moral or other regarding sentiments. It could be, they point out, that people who think that effort plays a major role in income generation are concerned about the incentive effects of taxation and oppose redistribution for this reason rather than because they doubt the "deservingness" of the poor (Piketty 1995). But I doubt that concerns about incentive costs fully explain attitudes towards redistribution. Were incentive costs of taxation the problem, those who believe that effort is important should support less government spending in general. Yet, as we show below, the belief that effort is important to getting ahead in life is negatively correlated with support for redistribution and positively correlated with support for military spending. If concerns about the incentive effects of taxation were the reason for opposition to redistribution, these individuals should also oppose the taxes that fund military expenditure. A quite different piece of evidence against the incentive-concerns interpretation is that subjects in a behavioral experiment on charitable giving to welfare recipients (described below) gave significantly more money when they were randomly paired with a welfare recipient who said she would like to work than when randomly paired with a welfare recipient who said she would not like to work (Fong 2007). There were no disincentive costs in this experiment, so some other interpretation is necessary.

This experimental result also addresses a second concern that economists have raised about the survey data: People who do not want to give to the poor for other reasons may say that the poor are lazy to justify their own selfishness. That is, the causal arrow runs from a preference not to help the poor to a belief about why the poor are not richer. This view is entirely consistent with the psychological theory of cognitive dissonance (Festinger 1957:602), but it cannot explain why randomly assigned treatment conditions in the charity experiment just described – pairing with a recipient predisposed to work or not – had significant effects on giving to welfare recipients.

It also could be that people whose income varies a lot from year to year come to believe that it is all a matter of luck, rather than hard work, but they may also (as we have seen in the previous chapter) vote for more redistribution simply as a self-interested insurance measure. Thus, the correlation between beliefs about the importance of luck vs. hard work and support for redistribution may not be causal; it may be the self-interest of the risk-exposed and risk-averse voter that explains support for redistribution. Showing why this concern is misplaced is a little more complicated; we will return to it after having introduced more of the relevant data.

Thus, we think that voters' concerns about the "undeserving poor" is an important aspect of the politics of redistribution. The concern is pronounced in the US, but is far from absent in Europe. Figure 5.1 shows that in twelve European countries those who say that poverty is caused by laziness are less concerned about poverty than the rest of the respondents by 0.42 of a standard deviation. In contrast, family income has a very modest effect. The differences in concern about poverty between the richest and poorest quartiles is less than a quarter as great as the difference between those who think that poverty is due to laziness and those who do not. The respondent's sex has a significant effect on concern about poverty independently of income and the other regressors, men being less concerned than women.

These results are extraordinarily robust: They do not depend on the particular sample and specification that we present. In all specifications, the effect of moving up to the next income quartile is an order of magnitude smaller than the effect of believing that poverty exists because the poor are lazy. When

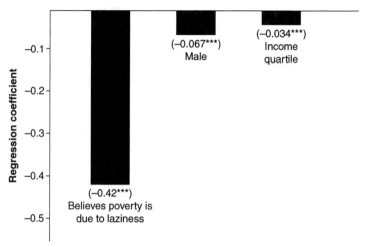

Figure 5.1 *Explaining concern about poverty: data from 12 European nations*
The data are from a Eurobarometer survey conducted in 1989 (Reif and Melich 1993). See Appendix for more details of measurement. Bars represent ordinary least squares coefficients (value of the estimated coefficient is in parentheses) predicting concern about poverty. The dependent variable is standardized so that the estimated coefficient represents the effect of the variable indicated on concern about poverty measured in standard deviation units. The equation also includes: age and country dummy variables. Significance levels are based on robust standard errors that allow for clustered errors within countries. This regression uses sample weights, although the results are not sensitive to them. There are 8,239 observations, $R^2=0.161$.
*** indicates significant at the 1% level.

one of the questions making up our composite measure of concern for the poor – asking whether or not the respondent thought that the public authorities are doing enough for the poor – was omitted, the effect of income was not even statistically significantly different from zero, regardless of whether other demographic variables were included in the regression, while the effect of beliefs that the poor are lazy remained large and highly significant.

I do not doubt that self-regarding motives often underpin apparently generous actions. Rather, we suggest that they do not always do so. Understanding egalitarian politics today requires a reconsideration of *Homo economicus*, the unremittingly self-regarding actor of economic theory. However, it would be a mistake to replace the textbook self-regarding actor with an equally one-dimensional altruistic actor willing to make unconditional, personally costly contributions to the less well-off. Instead, we believe that strong reciprocity, which involves *conditional* co-operation and punishment, better explains the motivations behind support for the welfare state.

As we will see, all three of our *personae* – *Homo economicus*, the strong reciprocator, and even the pure altruist – are represented in most groups of any size. For this reason, egalitarian policy-making, no less than the grand projects of constitutional design, risks irrelevance if it ignores the irreducible heterogeneity of human motivations. The problem of institutional design is not, as the classical economists thought, that uniformly self-regarding individuals be induced to interact in ways producing desirable aggregate outcomes, but rather that a mix of motives – self-regarding, reciprocal, and altruistic – interact in ways that prevent the self-regarding from exploiting the generous and hence unraveling co-operation when it is beneficial.

In the next section, I explain how individually costly but socially beneficial traits such as strong reciprocity can evolve in competition with self-regarding traits, when it might be expected that they would be eliminated by Darwinian competition.

The origins of strong reciprocity

Both historical and experimental evidence suggests that support for redistribution is often based on strong reciprocity motives. Consider first the historical evidence. In his *Injustice: The Social Bases of Obedience and Revolt*, my former teacher Barrington Moore sought to discern if there might be common motivational bases – "general conceptions of unfair and unjust behavior" (Moore 1978: 21) – for the moral outrage fueling struggles for justice that have recurred throughout human history. He concludes from his wide-ranging investigation that:

> There are grounds for suspecting that the welter of moral codes may conceal a certain unity of original form ... a general ground plan, a conception of what social relationships ought to be. It is a conception that by no means excludes hierarchy and authority, where exceptional qualities and defects can be the source of enormous admiration and awe. At the same time, it is one where services and favors, trust and affection, in the course of mutual exchanges, are ideally expected to find some rough balancing out. (4–5, 509)

Moore termed the general ground plan he uncovered "the concept of reciprocity – or better, mutual obligation, a term that does not imply equality of burdens or obligations" (506). In like manner, James Scott (1976) in his *Moral Economy of the Peasant* analyzed agrarian revolts, identifying violations of the "norm of reciprocity" as one of the essential triggers of insurrectionary motivations.

The experimental evidence reported below, as well as casual observation of everyday life, ethnographic and paleo-anthropological accounts of hunter-gatherer foraging bands from the late Pleistocene to the present (e.g. Boehm 2000), and historical narratives of collective struggles for democracy and justice (e.g. Wood 2003) have combined to convince me that strong reciprocity is a powerful and ubiquitous motive. But it is often objected that we must be mistaken, because natural selection would doom strong reciprocators and altruists alike to extinction, for both would be willing to sacrifice their fitness in order to help others.

Herbert Gintis and I have addressed this challenge in a decade-long research project culminating in our *A Co-operative*

Species: Human Reciprocity and Its Evolution (Bowles and Gintis 2011). I will just sketch our findings here. Strong reciprocity supports the adherence to norms within groups, and some of these norms – requiring work towards common ends, sharing, and monogamy, for example – are beneficial to most groups. Where reciprocity motivates the individually costly enforcement of these group-beneficial norms, strong reciprocity may evolve because the strong reciprocator will be disproportionately likely to be in groups that have effective norm adherence, and hence to enjoy the group benefits of these norms. By contrast, where reciprocity motivates the individually costly enforcement of norms that on average confer little benefit on group members, or inflict group costs, reciprocity is unlikely to evolve.

But our distant ancestors lived under conditions in which the group-level co-operation that strong reciprocators supported was a key to survival, for it allowed effective hunting of large animals, co-insurance among members of a band engaged in highly risky strategies of provision, and, most important, the successful defense against competing groups in the warfare that was then a major cause of death of young men and hence a key determinant of individual fitness (Bowles 2009). A key contributor to the evolutionary success of strong reciprocity, we think, was the common practice of sharing food with other members of one's group and other practices that resulted in what biologists term *reproductive leveling*, that is, smoothing out within group differences in fitness, and thereby attenuating the within-group fitness disadvantages which altruists (both unconditional and conditional) by definition suffered (Bowles 2006).

Strong reciprocity thus allows groups to engage in common practices without the resort to costly and often ineffective hierarchical authority, and thereby vastly increases the repertoire of social experiments capable of diffusing through cultural and genetic competition. The relevant traits may be transmitted genetically and proliferate under the influence of natural selection, or they may be transmitted culturally through learning from elders and age mates and proliferate because successful groups tend to absorb failing groups, or to be emulated by them. Gintis and I think it likely that both genetic and cultural transmission is involved. The 100,000-plus years in which anatomically modern humans lived primarily in foraging bands constitute a sufficiently long period, and a favorable social and physical ecology, for the genetic evolution of the combination of norm enforcement and sharing that we term strong reciprocity.

Experimental evidence

Behavioral experiments with human subjects provide over-whelming evidence against *Homo economicus*. Our first piece of evidence comes from the commonly observed rejection of substantial positive offers in ultimatum games. Experimental protocols differ, but the general structure of the ultimatum game is simple. Subjects are paired; one is the responder, the other the proposer. The proposer is provisionally awarded an amount ("the pie") to be divided between proposer and responder. The proposer offers a certain portion of the pie to the responder. If the responder accepts, the responder gets the proposed portion, and the proposer keeps the rest. If the responder rejects the offer, both get nothing. You do not have to be a game theorist to figure out that if you are the proposer, and you are just a selfish payoff maximizer, and you know that the respondent is just like you, then you should offer the respondent one penny, or the smallest positive amount permitted, knowing that it will be accepted (a penny beats nothing for a payoff maximizer).

But in experiments conducted with students in the United States, Slovakia, Japan, Israel, Slovenia, Germany, Russia, Indonesia, and more than 30 other countries, the vast majority of proposers offer between 40 percent and 50 percent of the pie, and offers lower than 20 percent of the pie are often rejected (Fehr and Schmidt 1999). These results have occurred in experiments with stakes as high as three months' earnings (Cameron 1999). With a group of anthropologists and economists I implemented ultimatum games in fifteen small-scale societies of Africa, Asia, and Latin America, not with students, but with hunter-gatherers, hand-tool farmers, and herders. In these societies, too, *Homo economicus* made an appearance, but was in a minority (Henrich, Boyd, Bowles *et al.* 2004, Henrich, Boyd, Bowles *et al.* 2005). Subsequent research with equally culturally diverse groups and with different experimental games supports the same conclusion (Herrmann, Thoni, and Gaechter 2008, Henrik, Ensminger, and McElreath *et al.* 2010).

When the ultimatum game proposers are asked why they offer more than 1 cent, proposers commonly say that they are afraid that respondents will consider low offers unfair and reject them as a way to punish their unwillingness to share. When respondents reject offers, they give virtually the same reasons for their actions. The proposers' actions might be explained by prudent self-interest, but the respondents' cannot. Because these behaviors occur in single-shot interactions and on the last round of multi-round interactions, they cannot be accounted for by the responder's attempt to modify subsequent behavior of the proposer. Punishment *per se* is the most likely motive. As evidence for this interpretation, we note that the rejection of positive offers is substantially less when the game is altered so that rejection does not punish the proposer (Abbink, Bolton, Sadrieh, and Tang 1996). Moreover, offers generated by a computer rather than another person are significantly less likely to be rejected (Blount 1995), suggesting that those rejecting low offers at a cost to themselves are reacting to violations of fairness norms rather than simply rejecting disadvantageous offers.

Punishment is triggered by responders' beliefs about the *intentions* of the proposer. This is shown clearly in an ultimatum game experiment in which the proposer has been provisionally given a $10 pie and has only two choices: either offer 2 (and hence keep 8) or make an alternative offer that varies across treatments in a way that allows the experimenters to test the effects of reciprocity and inequality-aversion on rejection rates (Falk, Fehr, and Fischbacher 2002). The alternative offers are 5 for the proposer and 5 for the responder (5/5), another is 2 for the proposer and 8 for the responder (2/8), and, finally, 10 for the proposer and 0 for the responder (10/0). When 5/5 is the alternative, the rejection rate of the 8/2 offer is 44.4 percent, significantly higher than the rejection rates in each of the other treatments. The most plausible interpretation of these results is that choosing a low offer when a fair one was possible suggests self-regarding intentions on the part of the proposer, which the responder often chooses to punish by rejecting the offer. (This experiment also found that 9 percent of 8/2 offers were rejected when the alternative offer was 10/0, indicating that some responders reject unequal outcomes at a personal cost, even when the proposer is in no sense responsible for the unequal situation.)

Our second piece of evidence comes from the simplest, but still quite revealing, laboratory experiment: the *dictator game*. In this game, one of two players, the "proposer," is given a sum of money, is asked to choose any part of the sum to give to the second player (the two players are mutually anonymous), and is permitted to keep the rest. *Homo economicus* gives nothing in this situation, whereas in actual experimental situations, a majority of proposers give positive amounts, typically ranging from 20 percent to 60 percent of the total (Forsythe, Horowitz, Savin, and Sefton 1994).

Using dictator games, researchers have shown that people are more generous to worthy recipients and bargaining partners. For example, Eckel and Grossman (1996) found that subjects in dictator games gave roughly three times as much when the recipient was the American Red Cross as when it was an anonymous subject. In the experiment mentioned at the outset, Fong (2007) conducted charity games (*n*-donor dictator games) in which several dictators were paired with a single real-life welfare recipient. The treatment conditions were randomly assigned and differed according to whether the welfare recipient expressed strong or weak work preferences on a survey that she completed. Dictators read the welfare recipients' surveys just prior to making their offers. Dictators who were randomly assigned to welfare recipients who expressed strong work preferences gave significantly more than dictators who expressed weak work preferences.

Additional evidence for strong reciprocity comes from *n*-player public goods experiments. The following is a common variant. Ten players are given $1 in each of ten rounds. In each round, each player can contribute any portion of the $1 (anonymously) to a "common pot." The experimenter divides the amount in the common pot by two, and gives *each* player that much money. If all ten players are co-operative, then on each round each puts $1 in the pot, the experimenter divides the $10 in the pot by two, and gives each player $5. After ten rounds of this, each subject has $50. By being self-regarding, however, each player can do better as long as the others are co-operating. By keeping the $1, the player ends up with "his" $10, and also receives $45 as his share of the pot, for a total of $55. If all behave this way, however, nobody contributes anything, and each ends up with only $10.

In fact, however, only a small fraction of players contribute nothing to the common pot. Rather, in the early stages of the game, people generally contribute half their money to the pot. In the later stages of the game, contributions decay until, at the end, they are contributing very little. Proponents of the *Homo economicus* model initially suggested that the reason for decay of public contribution is that participants really do not understand the game at first, and as they begin to learn it, they begin to realize the superiority of the free-riding strategy. However, there is considerable evidence that this interpretation is incorrect. For instance, Andreoni (1988) found that when the whole process is repeated with the same subjects, the initial levels of co-operation are restored, but once again co-operation decays as the game progresses, obviously contradicting the view that the decay was due to learning (could the subjects have "unlearned" what they learned in the first rounds of play when they started the second set?).

Andreoni (1995) suggested an explanation for the decay of co-operation quite suggestive of strong reciprocity: public-spirited contributors want to retaliate against free-riders, and the only way available to them in the game is by not contributing themselves. Indeed, if players are permitted to retaliate directly against non-contributors, but at a cost to themselves, they do so (Fehr and Gaechter 2000, Fehr and Gaechter 2002). In this situation, contributions rise in subsequent rounds to near the maximal level. Moreover, punishment levels are undiminished in the final rounds, suggesting that disciplining norm violators is an end in itself and, hence, will be exhibited even when there is no prospect of modifying subsequent shirking. This is strikingly shown in a similar experiment with a clever twist: In each round each subject was informed of the contribution levels of others and allowed to pay in order to dock other subjects' payoffs if they wished, but (here is the twist) the targets of the punishment would not be informed that they had been punished until the game was over (Fudenberg and Pathak 2010). Even knowing that it could have no effect on their targets' behavior, subjects avidly punished the free-riders.

Another result that is consistent with reciprocity is that co-operating and punishing behavior are very sensitive to the situation framing the interaction. In early research on what is known as *inequality aversion*, Loewenstein, Thompson, and Bazerman (1989) found that distributional preferences are sensitive to social context. They asked subjects to imagine themselves in various hypothetical situations. In one, the subject and another college student share the gains and losses from a jointly produced product. In another, the subject and a neighbor split the profit from selling a vacant lot between their homes. In a third, the subject is a customer dividing the proceeds from an expired rebate, or the cost of repairs, with a salesperson. They found, first, that subjects care about relative payoffs even more than they care about their absolute payoffs. Second, controlling for the subjects' own payoffs, earning less than the other person had a strong negative effect on utility in all situations and relationship types. However, an effect on utility of earning *more* than the other person (referred to as advantageous inequality) was also present, and depended on the relationship and the situation. Subjects disliked advantageous inequality if the relationship was friendly. However, if the relationship was unfriendly, advantageous inequality had little effect on their satisfaction level. Interestingly, they found that subjects preferred advantageous inequality in the customer/salesperson scenario, but disliked it in the other two scenarios (producing a product and splitting the proceeds from an empty lot).

Such experiments show that people do not like unfairness and are willing to incur a cost to punish those whom they perceive to have mistreated them (Ostrom, Walker, and Gardner 1992, Fehr, Gaechter, and Kirchsteiger 1997, Carpenter *et al.* 2009: 267). Impressed by this evidence for a more complex set of motivations featuring a strong aversion to unfairness, economists have produced new models stressing inequality aversion and reciprocity (Rabin 1993, Levine 1998, Fehr and Schmidt 1999).

Survey evidence

The experimental evidence applies directly to the politics of redistribution. Both unconditional altruists and strong reciprocators may support redistribution to the poor even if they stand no chance of ever benefitting materially as a result. Altruism is a widely discussed and important motive for assistance to the poor. But strong reciprocity provides a quite different perspective: Strong reciprocators wish to help those who try to make it on their own but who, for reasons beyond their own control, cannot, and they wish to punish, or withhold assistance from, those who are able but unwilling to work hard or who violate other social norms. At the outset we mentioned a number of objections to our interpretation based on the work of Fong (2001). Here is how Fong addressed them.

She used the 1998 Gallup Poll Social Audit Survey, "Haves and Have-Nots: Perceptions of Fairness and Opportunity," a randomly selected national sample in the US of 5,001 respondents. In each case she used the set of all individuals who responded to all of the questions used in the regression, unless noted otherwise. Relative to other commonly used surveys, the Gallup survey has a sample size large enough to allow statistical analysis with full controls for possibly confounding influences while focusing on narrow segments of the sample, namely, high-income and low-income sub-samples. Another attractive feature of this data source is its large number of measures that may capture self-interested reasons for one's opinions about redistribution, including not only the usual objective socio-economic variables like one's income, but also subjective measures of economic well-being and future expectations.

To construct a measure of support for redistribution Fong combined responses to five questions asking: if the government should "redistribute wealth by heavy taxes on the rich"; if the government should "make every possible effort to improve the ... position of the poor" or if instead the poor should "help themselves"; which organization "has the greatest responsibility for helping the poor: churches, private charities, the government, the families ... of poor people, the poor themselves, or someone else"; whether "money and wealth [should] be more evenly distributed"; and whether the gap between "rich" and "poor" is "a problem that needs to be fixed."

Two sets of measures of the causes of income are used in this study. The first contains two questions concerning the importance of effort and luck in causing wealth and poverty, and one question on whether or not there is plenty of opportunity to work hard and get ahead in America today. The second set is a series of questions about the importance of various factors, including race and sex, for getting ahead in life (see the appendix for this chapter for the wording of the questions, pp. 167–70). Self-interest as a possible motive for the respondents' opinions is measured by income and other variables likely to predict current and future tax obligations and current and future reliance on social insurance or redistribution programs. In Figures 5.2 and 5.3 Fong controlled for self-interest by including in the regressions income, race, sex, education, age, and the frequency with which respondents worry about meeting family expenses.

In Figure 5.2 I present results from her ordinary least squares regression that predicts support for redistribution using two sets of variables: beliefs about the causes of wealth and poverty and the measures of self-interest. To facilitate interpretation of the co-efficients, Fong standardized the dependent variable to have a zero mean and a standard deviation of one. The interpretation is as follows: Those who say that bad luck alone causes poverty are 0.50 of a standard deviation higher in their support for redistribution than those who think lack of effort alone causes poverty. Those who think that good luck alone causes wealth are 0.39 of a standard deviation higher on the support for redistribution scale than those who think effort alone causes wealth; and people who respond that there is plenty of opportunity in the US to get ahead scored 0.42 of a standard deviation lower in support for redistribution than people who do not think there is plenty of opportunity.

Measures of self-interest also have significant effects in the expected direction on support for redistribution. Those who are in the highest income category (annual household income

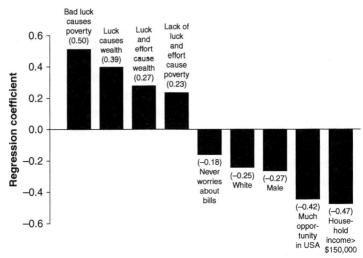

Figure 5.2 *Determinants of support for redistribution*
Bars represent ordinary least squares co-efficients (value of the
estimated coefficient is in parentheses) predicting support for
redistribution. The dependent variable is standardized so that
the estimated coefficient represents the effect of the variable
indicated on concern about poverty measured in standard
deviation units. The equation also includes seven additional
income dummies, age, a dummy for attended college, and
dummies for "worries about bills most of the time," "worries
about bills some of the time." The omitted category for household
income is less than $10,000 per year. The omitted categories for
causes of poverty and wealth are "lack of effort" and "strong
effort" respectively. To simplify the presentation of race effects,
we use the sample of white and black respondents only. Omitted
category for "worries about bills" is "all of the time." There are
3,417 observations. R^2=0.260. This regression uses sample
weights, although the results are not sensitive to them. We use
robust standard errors. All co-efficients are significant at the
1% level.

greater than $150,000) scored 0.47 of a standard deviation lower on support for redistribution than those in the lowest income category (income less than $10,000). Those who almost never worry about bills are significantly less supportive of redistribution than those who worry all of the time.

The effect of being white is large and highly significant, and the effect of being male is even larger: Controlling for income, beliefs about the causes of poverty, and other influences, white men are not very supportive of redistribution to the poor. The effect of race is mediated by beliefs about the characteristics of the poor, especially poor blacks.

Using ordered probit specifications to estimate similar equations (not shown here), Fong (2001) estimated the sizes of the effects of the independent variables on the probabilities of scoring in each of the six categories of the support-for-redistribution scale. In an equation that controls both for beliefs about the causes of wealth and poverty and for a large number of objective and subjective measures of and proxies for self-interest, the effects of being in the least privileged category (non-white, female, single, union member, part-time worker, no college education, in lowest income category, household size greater than four, and almost always worries about bills) as opposed to the most privileged are similar in size to the effects of believing that luck alone causes wealth and poverty as opposed to believing that effort alone causes wealth and poverty.

Let us return to the concern we raised at the outset: Maybe people who believe that poverty is caused by bad luck or circumstances beyond individual control are those who have high-variance incomes and who are, therefore, likely to benefit at least some of the time from the cushion provided by redistributive measures. So the belief is not causal; rather the highly variable nature of the respondent's economic fortunes are the true (and self-interested) reason why some people support redistribution. If this is correct, then the effect of these beliefs on redistributive policy preferences may have nothing to do with the psychology of holding the poor accountable and blaming them for their outcomes. It would simply be the case that beliefs about the causes of income are correlated with a person's financial position, which in turn determines his or her demand for redistribution.

If the beliefs about the causes of poverty and wealth operate through self-interest, then they should have no effect among people at the top and bottom of the distribution of income who expect to remain there. Those who do not expect to benefit should demand no redistribution at all, like people above the zero tax locus in Figure 4.3, regardless of their beliefs about the causes of income. Those who expect to benefit should register the highest degree of support for redistribution regardless of their beliefs about the causes of income. To test whether this is the case, Fong used sub-samples of: (1) individuals with incomes over $75,000 per year (that is, well over $100,000 in 2011 dollars) who expect to be better off in five years than they are today, and who do not worry about bills "all of the time"; (2) individuals with incomes under $10,000 per year; and (3) individuals with incomes under $30,000 per year who do not expect to be better off in five years than they are today, and who worry about bills more often than "almost never."

In all of these sub-samples, a quite inclusive set of measures capturing self-interest is jointly insignificant, meaning that one cannot reject the hypothesis that every single socio-economic variable has a coefficient of zero. Yet, the beliefs about roles of luck, effort, and opportunity in generating life outcomes were jointly significant for all three sub-samples. (The finding using ordered probit results are presented in Fong 2001.) Thus, among those who are poor and do not expect their lives to improve, those who believe that lack of effort causes poverty oppose redistribution. Analogously, support for redistribution is high among those securely well-off respondents who believe that poverty is the result of bad luck. So the finding is that people who think that the

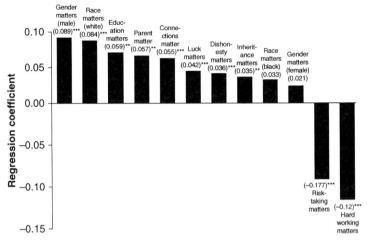

Figure 5.3 *Effects on the support for redistribution of respondents' beliefs in the importance of various factors for getting ahead in life*

Bars represent ordinary least squares coefficients (value of the estimated coefficient is in parentheses) predicting support for redistribution. The dependent variable is standardized. Independent variables are the respondent's belief in the importance of the factor shown to getting ahead in life (see Appendix for exact wording). The co-efficients are the estimated effects of a one-point increase in the response scale for a given belief on standard deviations of support for redistribution. Regressions also include all of the self-interest measures included in Figure 5.2, $R^2 = 0.184$. The number of observations was 3,437. This regression uses sample weights, although the results were not sensitive to them. ***Significant at the 1% level. **Significant at the 5% level.

vagaries of income are matters beyond their control support redistribution without thinking that they themselves will benefit from it.

In another test of self-interest, Fong used questions on the respondents' views on the importance of various factors, including a person's race and sex, in getting ahead in life. Figure 5.3 presents an ordinary least squares regression of respondents' support for redistribution on the importance of various determinants of success, while controlling for the same socio-economic variables included in the regression presented in Figure 5.2. Those who think that getting ahead is the rags-to-riches story of Horatio Alger, not surprisingly, do not like redistribution to the poor. Beliefs that "willingness to take risks" and "hard work and initiative" explain "why some people get ahead and succeed in life and others do not" have highly significant negative effects on support for redistribution. Beliefs that education, people's parents, connections, good luck, dishonesty, and inherited money explain why some people get ahead have significant positive effects on support for redistribution. But there is more, if you look carefully at Figure 5.2. Beliefs that a person's sex is important in getting ahead correlate positively with support for redistribution for both men and women, apparently because if this is the way the world works, then it is not fair and those who lose as a result should be compensated. But this is truer for men than for women. In fact, the effect of this belief for women is not only smaller than for men, but it is not significantly different from zero. Beliefs that a person's race is important in getting ahead in life have significant positive effects for whites, while the effect of these beliefs for blacks, though positive, is smaller and insignificant.

If people think that a person's race and sex are important to getting ahead in life, then the effects of these beliefs on self-interested demand for redistribution should operate in opposite directions for those who expect to benefit and those who expect to lose from racial or gender discrimination. In other words, whites who think race is important in getting ahead will expect to be economically advantaged and would have fewer self-interested reasons to support redistribution than whites who think that race does not matter. Similar reasoning holds for men who think a person's sex is important in getting ahead in life. This is more evidence that it is a sense of fairness, not self-interest, that is driving these results.

Concerns about the incentive effects of taxation are a final explanation for why people might oppose redistribution for reasons unrelated to any concern about the poor being undeserving. As we observed at the outset, this type of incentive concern should not apply only to redistribution, but to any tax-funded expenditure, including expenditures such as national defense. This is not what Fong found. Using the 1990 General Social Survey, Fong estimated ordered probit regressions predicting support for spending on welfare, national defense, halting the rising crime rate, and dealing with drug addiction, respectively (sample size ranges from 584 to 594). The independent variables are beliefs that the poor are poor because of lack of effort, and five demographic variables (income, education, race, sex, and age). In the samples reported above, the belief that lack of effort causes poverty has a highly significant negative effect on support for redistribution. However, the belief that lack of effort causes poverty does not lead to opposition to spending on crime or drug addiction, and these beliefs correlate positively with support for spending on defense. If these beliefs simply measure tax cost concerns, then their effect on support for all of these expenditure items should have been negative.

Opposition to redistribution reflects moral concerns going far beyond concerns about the poor being lazy. Heclo (1986) reported that 81 percent of survey respondents favor public funding for child care if the mother is a widow who is trying to support three children, while only 15 percent favor public funding when the mother has never married and is not interested in working.

Strong reciprocity and the welfare state: unhappy marriage?

While strong reciprocity may support egalitarianism, it may also help explain opposition to welfare state policies in some of the advanced market economies in the past decades, particularly since in the US, at least, such measures are believed by some to have promoted out-of-wedlock births and to have subsidized indolence. At the same time, it explains the continuing support for social security and Medicare in the US, since the public perception is that the recipients are "deserving," and the policies are thought not to support what are considered antisocial behaviors.

The cost – either in one's own taxes, or to the economy as a whole – is not the main source of opposition to such US programs as the former Aid to Families with Dependent Children, Food Stamps, and other means-tested social-support programs in the US. However, overwhelming majorities oppose the status quo, whatever their income, race, or personal history with such programs. This pattern of public sentiment, we think, can be accounted for in terms of the principle of strong reciprocity. While people generally overstate the share of the Federal budget devoted to welfare, this cannot account for the observed opposition: As a general rule, non-experts vastly overstate the share of the tax revenues devoted to things of which they disapprove, whether it be foreign aid, welfare, AIDS research, or military expenditure – the opposition is generally the cause of the exaggeration, not vice-versa. Farkas and Robinson (1996) note that in their sample of 1,000 Americans:

> By more than four to one (65% to 14%), Americans say the most upsetting thing about welfare is that "it encourages people to adopt the wrong lifestyle and values," not that "it costs too much tax money" ... Of nine possible reforms presented to respondents – ranging from requiring job training to paying surprise visits to make sure recipients deserve benefits – reducing benefits ranked last in popularity. (Farkas and Robinson 1996:9–10)

The cost, apparently, is not the problem. In focus groups, according to Farkas and Robinson, "Participants invariably dismissed arguments about the financial costs of welfare in almost derisive terms as irrelevant and beside the point" (Farkas and Robinson 1996:10).

Martin Gilens (1999) does not think that the opposition to the welfare state in the US is based on self-interest. He observes that "Politics is often viewed, by élites at least, as a process centered on the question 'who gets what.' For ordinary Americans, however, politics is more often about 'who *deserves* what' and the welfare state is no exception." In the Public Agenda data set used by Farkas and Robinson, respondents overwhelming considered welfare to be unfair to working people and addictive to recipients. By a more than five-to-one margin (69 percent to 13 percent overall, and 64 percent to 11 percent *for people receiving welfare*), respondents said that recipients abuse the system – for instance, by not looking for work. Moreover, 68 percent of respondents (and 59 percent of welfare recipients) thought that welfare is "passed on from generation to generation, creating a permanent underclass." In the same vein, 70 percent (71 percent of welfare recipients) said welfare makes it "financially better for people to stay on welfare than to get a job," 57 percent (62 percent of welfare recipients) thought welfare encourages "people to be lazy," and 60 percent (64 percent of welfare recipients) said the welfare system "encourages people to have kids out of wedlock." Note that the welfare recipients and other citizens hold similar views in this respect.

These objections to redistribution are moral, not self-interested, and they reflect a common normative framework and set of beliefs spanning those who receive transfers and those whose taxes finance them. That the respondents may hold exaggerated or simply false beliefs concerning the extent to which the welfare state is a cause of these behaviors is beside the point. Whether or not, for example, welfare *causes* out-of-wedlock births, for example, or fosters an unwillingness to work, citizens object to the system that provides financial support for those who undertake these socially disapproved behaviors. Their desire is to bear witness against the behavior and to disassociate themselves from it, whether or not their actions can change it.

Of course, racial stereotyping is part of the story, and here beliefs are not common across groups. The public agenda survey shows that whites are much more likely than African Americans to attribute negative attributes to welfare recipients, and much more likely to blame an individual's poverty on lack of effort. The survey data show, writes Gilens (1999:6), that:

> For most white Americans, race-based opposition to welfare is not fed by ill-will toward blacks, nor is it based on whites' desire to maintain their economic advantages over African Americans. Instead race-based opposition to welfare stems from the specific perception that, as a group, African Americans are not committed to the work ethic.

There is some evidence that people are more supportive of redistributions to their own ethnic and racial group. Erzo Luttmer (2001) found for a US sample that individuals are more opposed to welfare if they live in neighborhoods where a higher percentage of welfare recipients is of a different race.

Conclusion

It would not be difficult to design a system of income security and economic opportunity that would tap into rather than offend the altruism and reciprocity of today's citizens. Such a system would be generous towards the poor and rewarding those who perform socially valued but market-undervalued work, as well as towards those who are poor through accidents not of their own making, such as illness and job displacement. And it would guarantee unconditional access to basic goods such as health care and shelter, consistent with the widely documented motives of basic-needs generosity.

The task of politically viable egalitarian policy design might thus begin by identifying those actions that people believe entitle an individual to reciprocation. Of course, people's beliefs about what deserves reciprocation are not engraved in stone and often change when those who are not poor put themselves in the shoes of others, as has occurred for example to readers of Emile Zola's *Germinal* (1885) or Michael Harrington's *The Other America* (1962).

But egalitarian policy interventions need not await a change in citizens' beliefs about what kinds of thing deserve recipro-cation. Among these in the US today would be saving (when one's income allows), working hard both in schooling and on the job, and taking risks in productive endeavors. Persistent poverty is often the result of low returns on these socially admired behaviors: low wages for hard work, a low rate of return on savings, costly access to credit for those wishing to engage in uncertain entrepreneurial activities (or even outright credit-market exclusion), and educational environments so adverse as to frustrate even the most diligent student. Policies designed to raise the returns on these activities when under-taken by the less well-off would garner widespread support. A further principle of reciprocity-based egalitarian redistribution should be to insure individuals against the vagaries of bad luck without insuring them against the consequences of their own actions, particularly when these actions violate widely held social norms against such things as illicit drug use or child-bearing in the absence of reasonable guarantees of adequate parenting.

Like Pyotr Kropotkin (1989[1903]), the Russian biologist and author a century ago of the stirring manifesto for co-operation *Mutual Aid: A Factor in Evolution*, we find compelling evi-dence – both evolutionary and contemporary – for the force of human generosity and reciprocity. While many economists have failed to appreciate the practical importance of these predispositions in policy matters, their salience was not missed by Hayek (1978):

[The] demand for a just distribution ... is ... an atavism, based on primordial emotions. And it is these widely prevalent feelings to which prophets, [and] moral philosophers ... appeal by their plans for the deliberate creation of a new type of society. (18, 20)

If I am right, economists have misunderstood both the support for egalitarian redistribution and the revolt against the welfare state (where it has occurred), attributing the latter to selfishness by the electorate rather than the failure of many programs to tap powerful commitments to fairness and generosity that inspired Kropotkin and worried Hayek.

6

Conclusion: The new (not so dismal) science of inequality and redistribution

Good news often falls on deaf ears. In this case, my own. In 2002 I joined a campaign of trade unionists and community activists in Santa Fe, New Mexico, seeking an increase in the minimum wage, which, for the state of New Mexico, then stood at $4.15 an hour, well below the US federal minimum wage. When asked about the discrepancy, a Santa Fe businessman explained that it "sent a good signal to investors." Less than an hour into my first meeting with members of the so-called living-wage campaign, I found out that I, too, had become an equality pessimist.

The group was seeking an increase to $8.50 an hour. I balked, worried about the hotel room cleaners and restaurant food-choppers in this tourist town who might find themselves out of work. And I doubted whether the well-heeled, politically elite of the city would go for it. Couldn't we propose an increase to $5.50 and then, if we won, go on from there? A former organizer from the Communications Workers of America vociferously objected: "I'm not going to go out there and demand a wage that would place the worker below the poverty line even if she worked full time all year. I'm not going to sign on to that kind of injustice."

Suitably chastised, I set to work studying the likely job-loss effects of the proposed increase. A decade earlier I had responded to President Mandela's call for policies to expand employment, proposing a wage subsidy. James Heintz and

159

my econometric estimates using South African data indicated that it would make quite a dent on the unemployment problem there. I worried that similar reasoning, but in reverse, might apply in Santa Fe. If economists agree on anything, it is that raising the minimum wage will reduce employment, right? Economists hired by the hotels and restaurants told the City Council that this bad news was nothing less than a truism. But, as almost everybody who keeps up with the recent econometric literature now knows, this old chestnut is just not true, at least not for US labor markets (Card and Krueger 1995, Addison, Blackburn, and Cotti 2009, Dube, Lester, and Reich 2010, Allegretto, Dube, and Reich 2011).

In meetings of the City Council and over coffee with Council members, I outlined the new evidence from studies of employment in cities and states that had increased the minimum wage, for example comparing employment in fast-food outlets on opposite sides of a street delimiting jurisdictional boundaries. As a condition of her support, the key swing vote on the Council asked if we would agree to an independent evaluation of the employment effects a year after the implementation of the ordinance. We agreed, and the City Council enacted the ordinance in 2003. A year later, the investigation of the employment losses resulting from the wage hike, undertaken by the University of New Mexico Bureau of Business and Economic Research, came up empty-handed. They found none. In 2012 Santa Fe's minimum wage stood at $10.29 per hour, the highest in the US, and the former union organizer, David Coss, was a very popular second-term mayor of the City of Santa Fe.

It was time to listen to the good news and give up on equality pessimism.

Egalitarians have been successful in appealing to the more elevated human motives precisely when they have shown that the prevailing rules of the economic game violate norms of reciprocity, fairness, and compassion, and should be replaced by institutions that are more consistent with these norms and that also enhance living standards on the average. In the previous chapters I have provided the underlying logic for how this could be done. I have also explained how the extraordinary economic disparities now characteristic of the US and increasingly of other nations are a barrier to the adoption of productivity-enhancing economic institutions. This is the case because wealth redistribution is sometimes the only way to make less well-off people the owners of the fruits of their labors, their risk-taking, and, more broadly, of the consequences of their actions. Examples include land reform and employee ownership of their workplaces, as well as initiatives such as improved educational opportunity and policies to support home ownership. Similarly, an expansion of subsidies designed to promote employment and increase earnings among the poor, suggested by Edmund Phelps (1997), would tap into powerful reciprocity motives.

These policies of asset redistribution would need to be complemented by new forms of insurance to address the main downside of asset ownership for the less well-off, namely risk exposure, as we saw in Chapter 2. These could be reformulated along the lines suggested by John Roemer (1993) to protect individuals from risks over which they have no control, while not indemnifying people against the results of their own choices, other than providing a minimal floor to living standards. In this manner, for example, families could be protected against regional fluctuations in home values – the main form of wealth for most people – as Robert Shiller (1993) has shown. Other forms of insurance could partially protect workers from shifts in demand for their services induced by global economic changes. By reducing risk, these policies would greatly enhance the value to the less well-off of asset ownership – whether it be a home, the tools of one's trade, a cooperative workplace, or a high-quality education.

In Chapters 3 and 4 I showed how the globalization of production and the emerging rift between cosmopolitan and parochial citizens alters, but does not cramp, the space in which egalitarian political and economic initiatives must operate.

At the outset I asked, "Is egalitarianism passé?" I have now provided the reasons why I think not. A prominent reason to doubt equality pessimism, we have seen, is the cost of economic disparity: the blunted incentives of the wage worker, the exclusion of the would-be entrepreneur from credit markets, the impediments to trust and mutual concern essential to finding co-operative solutions to workplace, neighborhood, and global problems, and the mounting cost of containing the conflicts endemic to a society of haves and have-nots.

Other reasons are less readily calibrated in the economic costs of inequality, but are no less real. Mounting income inequality is among the reasons why (in all countries for which we have adequate data) the historic decline in working hours slowed and, in some countries, ground to a halt in the fourth quarter of the last century (Bowles and Park 2005, Oh, Park, and Bowles 2012). Keeping up with the Jones' required more hours on the job as the Jones' incomes became stratospheric. The result over the final quarter of the past century was an increase in annual working time of production workers not only in the US, but also in Sweden. The costs: not only fewer hours for family, friends, and civic pursuits, but a lifestyle tilted towards commodities rather than free time, and a fateful trajectory that heightens resource use and environmental degradation. A program of productivity-enhancing asset redistribution would contribute to an environmentally sustainable future by making output per hour of work – not total output – the target of economic policy, and thereby valuing free time while attenuating the rat-race dynamic of keeping up with the Jones'. Reducing wealth disparities would also level the political playing-field not only for environmental policies (Boyce 2007) but across the board.

Recent developments in economics – the twin revolutions in the theory of contracts and the behavioral assumptions of the discipline on which the previous chapters are based – provide little support for the equality pessimism I discussed at the outset, even in a world of global mobility of goods, capital, and people. The political impediments to egalitarian redistribution are daunting. But there is nothing in human nature or the inexorable logic of the once-dismal science that now stands in the way of redistributing wealth more equally, giving citizens a more equal voice in their workplaces, neighborhoods and nations, and taking a step in the direction of what radical egalitarians have dreamed of: a society of real freedom for all.

Appendices

Notation for derivatives

If $x = f(y)$, then $x' \equiv \frac{dx}{dy}$ and $x'' \equiv \frac{d^2 x}{dy^2}$

If $x = f(y, z)$, then $f_y \equiv \frac{\partial x}{\partial y}$ and $f_z \equiv \frac{\partial x}{\partial z}$

Appendix to Chapter 3

The model and notation

(1)	$Q = yhe(1 - m)$ for $K \geq kh(1 - m)$	production
	$= 0$ for $K < kh(1 - m)$	capital requirement
(2)	$w^* = a/\tau(1 - h) + b$	labor supply
		equilibrium cond.
(3)	$\pi = r(1 - t) = \dfrac{(1 - t)[(y - k)h(1 - m) - hw]}{[kh(1 - m)]}$	after-tax profit rate
(4)	$\pi = \rho\mu$	stationary K
(5)	$\underline{w} = (1 - m)\left(\dfrac{y - k(1 + \rho\mu)}{(1 - t)}\right)$	labor demand
		equilibrium cond.
(6)	$w^* = \underline{w}$	equilibrium in
		national economy
(7)	$b(1 - h) + p = th([(1 - m)y(\lambda p) - k] - w)$	government budget
		constraint
(8)	$\omega = (1 - m^-)\left(\dfrac{y(\sigma^-) - k(1 + \rho\mu)}{(1 - t)}\right)$	exp. residual claim of
		co-op members

Notation

y	output per unit of effort
h	hours employed (labor demand)
m	monitoring (fraction of labor time)
k	capital per hour of productive labor
w^*	no shirking wage
a	disutility of effort
τ	probability of detection (shirker) and termination
b	terminated workers' fallback
π	after-tax profit rate
t	profits tax rate
μ	risk premium $(=1/(1-c))$
c	probability of confiscation
ρ	risk-free interest rate
s	ratio of labour supply to adult population
λ	effectiveness of public expenditure
p	level of public investment
ω	expected residual claim (co-op)
σ	st. dv. of members' income stream
u	co-op members' utility

The no-shirking wage

The no-shirking wage equates the payoff to working (the wage minus the disutility of providing $e = 1$) with the expected payoff to not working, which is the sum of three terms capturing the three things that may occur for the person who supplies $e = 0$. These are: with probability $1 - \tau$ one is not terminated and so receives the wage w; with probability τ one is fired, in which case one of two things could occur. Either one finds another job, which occurs (we will assume for simplicity) with probability h (the fraction of the labor force employed), or one does not find a job (occurring with probability $1 - h$) and then receives the income-replacing payment b. Thus, the smallest wage consistent with the worker supplying $e = 1$ is given by:

$$w - a = (1 - \tau) + \tau hw + \tau(1 - h)b$$

which means that (rearranging) the no-shirking wage is:

$$w^* = \frac{a}{\tau(1 - h)} + b$$

Appendix to Chapter 4

To take account of the financing of the BIG we let the citizen pay a tax equal to a fraction τ of her income and receive a grant of b, with the two terms selected so that varying the size of the grant and its necessary funding does not alter the citizen's expected income. (This is just a device for abstracting from the redistributive effects of the BIG so as to study the pure insurance effects.) Given some tax rate (t) and grant (b), when the citizen selects a level of risk σ, and language training λ measured in standard deviation units of risk reduction, her realized income (taking account of both the BIG and the cost of learning the lingua franca) is:

$$y = (g(\underline{\sigma}) + z\underline{\sigma})(1 - t) + b - f\lambda$$

and the realized standard deviation of income is $\sigma = \underline{\sigma}(1 - t) - \lambda$. From this latter expression we see that a larger BIG (financed by a larger t) reduces the risk exposure of the citizen. Writing $g(\underline{\sigma}, \lambda)$ for the citizen's expected income (just the above expression for realized income minus the $z\underline{\sigma}$ term), the citizen varies $\underline{\sigma}$ and λ to maximize $v = v[g(\sigma, \lambda), \sigma(\sigma, \lambda)]$. This optimization problem gives us the tangency conditions shown in the text, namely $f = g' = -v_\sigma / v_g$, requiring that the two marginal rates of transformation of risk into expected income be equal to the marginal rate of substitution between risk and expected income (that is, the citizen's degree of risk aversion).

The assumption that, for a given cost (of lingua franca learning), the realized standard deviation of income can be reduced by a given amount simplifies the model (it makes the cultural risk-reduction technology linear), but does not account for the results. Were I to assume more realistically that the costs of further risk reduction are greater as risk exposure is reduced, the results presented here would be strengthened (for example, entirely eliminating the incentive to learn a lingua franca would require a smaller BIG than is shown in Figure 4.7).

Appendix to Chapter 5

Table 5.1

The data are from a Eurobarometer survey conducted in 1989 (Reif and Melich 1993), representative of the population aged 15 and over in the twelve European Union countries of that time. Of the data set's 11,819 respondents, we use the 8,239 who answered all of the questions included in our analysis. Our dependent variable is the sum of responses to four questions about the importance of fighting unemployment (1) and poverty (2), the importance of reducing differences between regions within the country by helping regions that are less developed or in difficulties (3), and whether the public authorities in the country do all that they should for poor people (4). The measure increases in concern about poverty, unemployment, and inequality and the belief that the public authorities do not "do enough for poor people." For simplicity, we refer to this composite measure as "concern about poverty." Our independent variable of primary interest is the belief that poverty is caused by laziness rather than being caused by bad luck, injustice, or no reason at all, or that poverty is inevitable. The other variables included in the regression are family income quartiles, sex, and age. Note that item (4) in our dependent variable is explicitly country-specific.

Cross-country comparisons of a question like this are of little value because people in a country with a generous redistribution system may care very much about poverty, but believe that their own government is doing a good job of addressing it. The other three items used to construct our dependent measure are subject to the same concern, albeit to a lesser extent. To account for the effects of unmeasured differences between countries, we use fixed effects to allow for country differences in mean responses.

Support for redistribution variable from the Gallup Survey

The dependent variable was constructed on the basis of the following questions:

1. People feel differently about how far a government should go. Here is a phrase which some people believe in and some don't. Do you think our government should or should not redistribute wealth by heavy taxes on the rich? (Response categories: should, should not)
2. Some people feel that the government in Washington, DC should make every possible effort to improve the social and economic position of the poor. Others feel that the government should not make any special effort to help the poor, because they should help themselves. How do you feel about this? (Response categories: government should help the poor, the poor should help themselves)
3. Which one of the following groups do you think has the greatest responsibility for helping the poor: churches, private charities, the government, the families and relatives of poor people, the poor themselves, or someone else? (Response categories: groups other than the poor, the poor themselves)
4. Do you feel that the distribution of money and wealth in this country today is fair, or do you feel that the money

and wealth in this country should be more evenly distributed among a larger percentage of the people? (Response categories: distribution is fair, should be more evenly distributed)

5. Do you think that the fact that some people in the United States are rich and others are poor (1) represents a problem that needs to be fixed or (2) is an acceptable part of our economic system? (Response categories: problem, acceptable)

The questions on the General Social Survey read as follows:

1. Plenty of opportunity in the US: Some people say that there's not much opportunity in America today, that the average person doesn't have much chance to really get ahead. Others say there's plenty of opportunity and anyone who works hard can go as far as they want. Which one comes closer to the way you feel about this? (1) Not much opportunity (2) Plenty of opportunity

2. Causes of poverty: Just in your opinion, which is more often to blame if a person is poor – lack of effort on his or her part, or circumstances beyond his or her control? (1) Lack of effort (2) Both (3) Luck or circumstances beyond his/her control

3. Causes of wealth: Just in your opinion, which is more often to blame if a person is rich – strong effort on his or her part, or circumstances beyond his or her control? (1) Strong effort (2) Both (3) Luck or circumstances beyond his/her control

4. Determinants of success: I am going to read several reasons why some people get ahead and succeed in life and others do not. Using a one-to-five scale, where "1" means not at all important and "5" means extremely important, please tell me how important it is as a reason for a person's success. You can choose any number from one to five. A: How important are willingness to take risks? B: How important is money inherited from families?

C: How important is hard work and initiative? D: How important is ability or talent that a person is born with? E: How important is dishonesty and willingness to take what they can get? F: How important is good luck, being in the right place at the right time? G: How important are parents and the family environment they grow up in? H: How important is physical appearance and good looks? I: How important is [sic] connections and knowing the right people? J: How important is being a member of a particular race or ethnic group? K: How important is getting the right education or training? L: How important is a person's gender, that is whether they are male or female?

Works cited

Abbink, K., G. E. Bolton, A. Sadrieh, and F.-F. Tang. 1996. "Adaptive Learning versus Punishment in Ultimatum Bargaining." Discussion paper no. B-381. Rheinische: Friedrich-Wilhelms-Universität Bonn.

Acemoglu, Daron, Simon Johnson, and James Robinson. 2005. "Institutions as the Fundamental Cause of Long-Growth," in *Handbook of Economic Growth.* Philippe Aghion and Steven Durlauf eds. Amsterdam: North-Holland.

Acemoglu, Daron and James Robinson. 2012. *Why Nations Fail: The Origins of Power, Prosperity and Poverty.* Crown: 2011.

Addison, John T., McKinley L. Blackburn, and Chad Cotti. 2009. "New Estimates of the Effects of Minimum Wages in the U.S. Retail Trade Sector." *Labour Economics* **16**:4, 397–408.

Alchian, Armen A. and Harold Demsetz. 1972. "Production, Information Costs, and Economic Organization." *American Economic Review* **62**:5, 777–95.

Alesina, A., E. Glaeser, and B. Sacerdote. 2001. "Why Doesn't the United States Have a European-Style Welfare State." *Brookings Papers on Economic Activity* **2**, 187–278.

Alesina, Alberto and Dani Rodrik. 1994. "Distributive Politics and Economic Growth." *Quarterly Journal of Economics* **109**, 465–90.

Allegretto, Sylvia, Arindrajit Dube, and Michael Reich. 2011. "Do Minimum Wages Really Reduce Teen Employment? Accounting for Heterogeneity and Selectivity in State Panel Data." *Industrial Relations* **50**:5, 205–40.

172 **Works cited**

Anand, S. and R. Kanbur. 1991. "Public Policy and Basic Needs Provision: Intervention and Achievement in Sri Lanka," in *The Political Economy of Hunger: Vol. III: Endemic Hunger.* J. Drèze and A. Sen eds. Oxford: Clarendon Press.

Andreoni, James. 1988. "Why Free Ride? Strategies and Learning in Public Good Experiments." *Journal of Public Economics* **37**, 291–304.

1995. "Cooperation in Public Goods Experiments: Kindness or Confusion." *American Economic Review* **85**:4, 891–904.

Ardington, Elisabeth and Frances Lund. 1995. "Pensions and Development: Social Security as Complementary to Programs of Reconstruction and Development." *Southern Africa* **12**:4, 557–77.

Arrow, Kenneth J. 1971. "Political and Economic Evaluation of Social Effects and Externalities," in *Frontiers of Quantitative Economics.* M. D. Intriligator ed. Amsterdam: North-Holland, 3–23.

Asplund, Marcus. 2000. "What Fraction of a Capital Investment is Sunk Costs." *Journal of Industrial Economics* **48**:3, 287–303.

Atkinson, A. 1999. "Equity Issues in a Globalizing World: The Experience of the OECD Countries," in *Economic Policy and Equity.* Vito Tanzi, Ke-Young Chu and Sanjeev Gupta eds. Washington: International Monetary Fund, pp. 63–98.

Atkinson, Anthony, Thomas Piketty, and Emmanuel Saez. 2011. "Top Incomes in the Long Run of History." *Journal of Economic Literature* **49**:1, 3–71.

Baker, G. and T. Hubbard. 2000. "Contractibility and Asset Ownership: On-Board Computers and Governance in US Trucking." Issue 7634 of Working Paper series. Cambridge, MA: National Bureau of Economic Research.

Banerjee, Abhijit and Esther Duflo. 2010. "Giving Credit Where it is Due." *Journal of Economic Perspectives* **24**: 61–79.

2011. *Poor Economics: A Radical Rethinking of the Way to Fight Global Poverty.* New York: Public Affairs Books.

Banerjee, Abhijit, Paul J. Gertler, and Maitreesh Ghatak. 2002. "Empowerment and Efficiency: Tenancy Reform in West Bengal." *Journal of Political Economy* **110**:2, 239–80.

Bardhan, Pranab and John Roemer. 1992. "Market Socialism: A Case for Rejuvenation." *Journal of Economic Perspectives* **6**:3, 101–16.

Bardhan, Pranab, Samuel Bowles, and Herbert Gintis. 2000. "Wealth Inequality, Credit Constraints, and Economic Performance," in *Handbook of Income Distribution*. Anthony Atkinson and François Bourguignon eds. Dortrecht: North-Holland, pp. 541–603.

Bardhan, Pranab, Samuel Bowles, and Michael Wallerstein. 2005. *Globalization and Egalitarian Redistribution*. Princeton and New York: Princeton University Press and Russell Sage Foundation.

Belloc, Marianna and Samuel Bowles. 2012. *International Trade and the Persistence of Cultural-Institutional Diversity*. Working Paper. Santa Fe Institute.

Besley, T. and R. Burgess. 1998. "Land Reform, Poverty Reduction and Growth: Evidence From India." *Development Economics Discussion Paper Series* 13. London School of Economics, The Suntory Centre.

Besley, T. and S. Coate. 1992. "Understanding Welfare Stigma: Taxpayer Resentment and Statistical Discrimination." *Journal of Public Economics* **48**:1, 165–83.

Binswanger, H. P. 1980. "Attitudes Towards Risk: Experimental Measurements in Rural India." *American Journal of Agricultural Economics* **62**(August), 395–407.

Black, Jane, David de Meza, and David Jeffreys. 1996. "House Prices, the Supply of Collateral and the Enterprise Economy." *Economic Journal* **106**:434, 60–75.

Blanchflower, David and Andrew Oswald. 1998. "What Makes a Young Entrepreneur?" *Journal of Labor Economics* **16**:1, 26–60.

Blount, Sally. 1995. "When Social Outcomes Aren't Fair: The Effect of Causal Attributions on Preferences." *Organizational Behavior and Human Decision Processes* **63**:2, 131–44.

Boehm, Christopher. 2000. *Hierarchy in the Forest*. Cambridge, MA: Harvard University Press.

Bordo, A., A. Taylor, and Jeffrey Williamson eds. 2003. *Globalization in Historical Perspective*. University of Chicago Press.

Bourguignon, F. 2012. *La mondialisation de l'inégalité*. Paris: Editions du Seuil.

Bourguignon, F. and C. Morrison. 2002. "Inequality Among World Citizens: 1820–1992." *American Economic Review* **92**:4, 727–44.

Bowles, Samuel. 1992. "Is Income Security Possible in a Capitalist Economy? An Agency Theoretic Analysis of an Unconditional Income Grant." *European Journal of Political Economy* **8**, 557–78.

  2004. *Microeconomics: Behavior, Institutions, and Evolution.* Princeton University Press.

  2006. "Group Competition, Reproductive Leveling and the Evolution of Human Altruism." *Science* **314**, 1569–72.

  2009. "Did Warfare among Ancestral Hunter-Gatherer Groups Affect the Evolution of Human Social Behaviors?" *Science* **324**, 1293–98.

  2012. "My dinner party with Karl, Leon and Maynard: A one-act play in seven scenes in honor of the life and work of Tom Weisskopf," in *Capitalism on Trial: Explorations in the Tradition of Thomas Weisskopf.* Jeannette Wicks-Lim and Robert Pollin eds. Cheltenham: Edward Elgar.

Bowles, Samuel and Robert Boyer. 1988. "Labor Discipline and Aggregate Demand: A Macroeconomic Model." *American Economic Review* **78**:2, 395–400.

  1990. "Labor Market Flexibility and Decentralization as Barriers to High Employment? Notes on Employer Collusion, Centralized Wage Bargaining and Aggregate Employment," in *Labour Relations and Economic Performance.* Renato Brunetta and Carlo Dell'Aringa eds. London: Macmillan.

  1995. "Wages Aggregate Demand and Employment in an Open Economy: A Theoretical and Empirical Investigation," in *Macroeconomic Policy after the Conservative Era: Research on Investment Savings and Finance.* Gerald Epstein and Herbert Gintis eds. Cambridge University Press.

Bowles, Samuel and Herbert Gintis. 2011. *A Cooperative Species: Human Reciprocity and its Evolution.* Princeton University Press.

Bowles, Samuel and Arjun Jayadev. 2007. "Garrison America." *The Economists' Voice* **4**:2, Article 3.

Bowles, Samuel and Ugo Pagano. 2006. "Economic Integration, Cultural Standardization, and the Politics of Social Insurance," in *Globalization and Egalitarian Redistribution.* Samuel Bowles, Pranab Bardhan and Michael Wallerstein (eds.), Princeton University Press.

Bowles, Samuel and Yong-Jin Park. 2005. "Inequality, Emulation, and Work Hours: Was Thorsten Veblen Right?" *Economic Journal* **15**, F397–F413.

Bowles, Samuel, David M. Gordon, and Thomas E. Weisskopf. 1990. *After the Waste Land: A Democratic Alternative for the Year 2000*. Armonk, NY: M. E. Sharpe.

Boyce, James. 2007. "Inequality and Environmental Protection." in *Inequality, Co-operation and Environmental Protection*. J. M. Baland, Pranab Bardhan, and Samuel Bowles eds. Princeton University Press.

Cameron, L. A. 1999. "Raising the Stakes in the Ultimatum Game: Experimental Evidence from Indonesia." *Economic Inquiry* **37**:1, 47–59.

Card, David and Alan B. Krueger. 1995. *Myth and Measurement: The New Economics of the Minimum Wage*. Princeton University Press.

Carpenter, Jeffrey, Samuel Bowles, Herbert Gintis, and Sung-Ha Hwang. 2009. "Strong Reciprocity and Team Production: Theory and Evidence." *Journal of Economic Behavior and Organization* **71**:2, 221–32.

Carter, Michael, Bradford Barham, and Dina Mesbah. 1996. "Agricultural Export Booms and the Rural Poor in Chile, Guatemala and Paraguay." *Latin American Research Review* **31**:1, 33–65.

Choi, Minsik. 2004. "The Threat Effect of Capital Mobility on Wage Bargaining," in Bardhan, Bowles, and Wallerstein eds.

Cohen, G. A. 2009. *Why Not Socialism?* Princeton University Press.

D'Antoni, M. and Ugo Pagano. 2002. "National Cultures and Social Protection as Alternative Insurance Devices." *Structual Change and Economic Dynamics* **13**, 367–86.

D'Azeglio, Massimo. 1867. *I miei ricordi*. Turin: Taparelli.

Demsetz, Harold and Kenneth Lehn. 1985. "The Structure of Corporate Control: Causes and Consequences." *Journal of Political Economy* **93**:6, 1155–77.

Domar, Evsey and Richard A. Musgrave. 1944. "Proportional Income Taxation and Risk-Taking." *Quarterly Journal of Economics* **58**, 388–422.

Dube, Arindrajit, William Lester, and Michael Reich. 2010. "Minimum Wage Effects across State Borders: Estimates Using Contiguous Counties." *Review of Economics and Statistics* **92**:4, 945–64.

Dugatkin, L. A. 2011. *The Prince of Evolution*. N/p: Createspace.

Eckel, Catherine and Philip Grossman. 1996. "Altruism in Anonymous Dictator Games." *Games and Economic Behavior* **16**, 181–91.

Evans, David and Boyan Jovanovic. 1989. "An Estimated Model of Entrepreneurial Choice under Liquidity Constraints." *Journal of Political Economy* **97**:4, 808–27.

Falk, A., E. Fehr, and U. Fischbacher. 2002. *Testing Theories of Fairness and Reciprocity-Intentions Matter*. University of Zurich.

Farkas, Steve and Jean Robinson. 1996. *The Values We Live by: What Americans Want from Welfare Reform*. New York: Public Agenda.

Fehr, Ernst and Simon Gaechter. 2000. "Fairness and Retaliation: The Economics of Reciprocity." *Journal of Economic Perspectives* **14**:3, 159–81.

  2002. "Altruistic Punishment in Humans." *Nature* **415**, 137–40.

Fehr, Ernst and Klaus M. Schmidt. 1999. "A Theory of Fairness, Competition, and Cooperation." *Quarterly Journal of Economics* **114**:3, 817–68.

Fehr, Ernst, Simon Gaechter, and Georg Kirchsteiger. 1997. "Reciprocity as a Contract Enforcement Device: Experimental Evidence." *Econometrica* **65**:4, 833–60.

Festinger, Leon. 1957. *A Theory of Cognitive Dissonance*. Stanford University Press.

Fong, Christina. 2001. "Social Preferences, Self-Interest and the Demand for Redistribution." *Journal of Public Economics* **82**:2, 225–46.

  2007. "Evidence from an Experiment on Charity to Welfare Recipients: Reciprocity, Altruism and the Empathic Responsiveness Hypothesis." *Economic Journal* July. 117 (522), 1008–24.

Fong, Christina, Samuel Bowles, and Herbert Gintis. 2005. "Strong Reciprocity and the Welfare State," in *Handbook of Giving. Reciprocity and Altruism*. Serge-Christophe Kolm and Jean Mercier Ythier eds. Amsterdam: Elsevier.

Forsythe, Robert, Joel Horowitz, N.E. Savin, and Martin Sefton. 1994. "Replicability, Fairness and Pay in Experiments with Simple Bargaining Games." *Games and Economic Behavior* **6**:3, 347–69.

Freeman, R. and J. Medoff. 1984. *What Do Unions Do?* New York: Basic Books.

Fudenberg, Drew and Parag Pathak. 2010. "Unobserved Punishment Supports Co-operation." *Journal of Public Economics* **94**, 78–86.

Gallup. 1998. "Haves and Have-Nots: Perceptions of Fairness and Opportunity." *Gallup News Organization* (July 6), 1–34.

Garrett, Geoffrey. 1998. *Partisan Politics in the Global Economy.* Cambridge University Press.

Gellner, Ernest. 1983. *Nations and Nationalism.* Ithaca: Cornell University Press.

Gilens, Martin. 1999. *Why Americans Hate Welfare.* University of Chicago Press.

Glaeser, Edward and Denise DiPasquale. 1999. "Incentives and Social Capital: Are Homeowners Better Citizens." *Journal of Urban Economics* **45**:2, 354–84.

Glyn, Andrew. 2006. *Capitalism Unleashed.* Oxford University Press.

Glyn, Andrew and Robert Sutcliffe. 1999. "Still Underwhelmed: Indicators of Globalization and their Misinterpretation." *Review of Radical Political Economy* **31**:1, 111–32.

Glyn, Andrew, Alan Hughes, Alain Lipietz, and Ajit Singh. 1990. "The Rise and Fall of the Golden Age," in *The Golden Age of Capitalism: Reinterpreting the Postwar Experience.* Stephen Marglin and Juliet B. Schor eds. Oxford: Clarendon Press, pp. 39–125.

Gordon, David M. 1994. "Bosses of Different Stripes: A Cross-National Perspective on Monitoring and Supervision." *American Economic Review* **84**:2, 375–79.

1998. "The Global Economy: New Edifice or Crumbling Foundations." *New Left Review* **68**, 24–64.

Green, Leonard, Joel Myerson, David Lichtman, Suzanne Rosen, and Astrid Fry. 1996. "Temporal Discounting in Choice Between Delayed Rewards: The Role of Age and Income." *Psychology and Aging* **11**:1, 79–84.

Gross, David and Nicholas Souleles. 2002. "Do Liquidity Constraints and Interest Rates Matter for Consumer Behavior? Evidence From Credit Card Data." *Quarterly Journal of Economics* **117**:1, 149–85.

Guiso, Luigi, T. Jappelli, and D. Terlizzese. 1996. "Income Risk, Borrowing Constraints, and Portfolio Choice." *American Economic Review* **86**:1, 158–72.

Hall, Peter and David Soskice. 2001. *Varieties of Capitalism: The Institutional Foundations of Comparative Advantage.* Oxford University Press.

Hausman, Jerry. 1979. "Individual Discount Rates and the Purchase and Utilization of Energy-using Durables." *Bell Journal of Economics* **10**:1, 33–54.

Hayek, Frederick. 1978. *The Three Sources of Human Values.* London School of Economics.

Heclo, H. 1986. "The Political Foundations of Antipoverty Policy," in *Fighting Poverty: What Works and What Doesn't.* Sh. H. Danziger and D. H. Weinberg eds. Cambridge, MA: Harvard University Press, pp. 312–41.

Henrich, Joe, Robert Boyd, Sammel Bowles, Ernst Fehr, Colin Camerer, and Herbert Gintis. 2004. *Foundations of Human Sociality: Economic Experiments and Ethnographic Evidence in 15 Small-Scale Societies.* Oxford University Press.

Henrich, Joseph, Robert Boyd, Samuel Bowles, Colin Camerer, Ernst Fehr, Herbert Gintis, Richard McElreath, Michael Alvard, Abigail Barr, Jean Ensminger, Kim Hill, Francisco Gil-White, Michael Gurven, Frank Marlowe, John Q. Patton, Natalie Smith, and David Tracer. 2005. "'Economic Man' in Cross-Cultural Perspective: Behavioral Experiments in 15 Small-Scale Societies." *Behavioral and Brain Sciences* **28**, 795–855.

Henrik, Joseph, Jean Ensminger, Richard McElreath, Abigail Barr, Clark Barrett, Alexander Bolyanatz, Juan Camilo Cardenas, Michael Gurven, Edwins Gwako, Natalie Herich, Carolyn Lesogorol, Frank Marlowe, David Tracer, and John Ziker. 2010. "Markets, Religion, Community Size, and the Evolution of Fairness and Punishment." *Science* **327**, 1480–84.

Herrmann, Benedikt, Christian Thoni, and Simon Gaechter. 2008. "Antisocial Punishment across Societies." *Science* **319**:7 (March), 1362–67.

Holtz-Eakin, Douglas, David Joulfaian, and Harvey S. Rosen. 1994. "Sticking it out: Entrepreneurial Survival and Liquidity Constraints." *Journal of Political Economy* **102**:1, 53–75.

Huber, E. and J. Stephens. 1998. "Internationalization and the Social Democratic Model." *Comparative Political Studies* **31**:3, 353–97.

Isenman, P. 1980. "Basic Needs: The Case of Sri Lanka." *World Development* **8**:3, 237–58.

Iversen, Torben and David Soskice. 2001. "An Asset Theory of Social Policy Preferences." *American Political Science Review* **95**:4, 875–93.

Jappelli, Tullio. 1990. "Who is Credit Constrained in the US Economy." *Quarterly Journal of Economics* **105**:1, 219–34.

Jarvis, Lovell. 1989. "The Unraveling of Chile's Agrarian Reform, 1973–1986," in *Searching for Agrarian Reform in Latin America*. William Thiesenhusen ed. Boston: Unwin-Hyman, pp. 240–65.

Jayadev, Arjun and Samuel Bowles. 2005. "Guard Labor." *Journal of Development Economics* **79**, 328–48.

Kerr, Benjamin, Peter Godfrey-Smith, and Marcus Feldman. 2004. "What is Altruism?" *Trends in Ecology and Evolution* **19**:3, 135–40.

Keynes, J. M. 1933. "National Self-Sufficiency." *Yale Review* **22**, 755–69.

Kindleberger, Charles P. 1969. *American Business Abroad: Six Lectures on Direct Investment*. New Haven: Yale University Press.

Kolm, Serge-Christophe. 1984. *La Bonne Economie: La réciprocité général*. Paris: Presses Universitaires de France.

Kropotkin, Peter. 1989 [1903]. *Mutual Aid: A Factor in Evolution*. New York: Black Rose Books.

Laffont, Jean Jacques. 2000. *Incentives and Political Economy*. Oxford University Press.

Laffont, Jean Jacques and Mohamed Salah Matoussi. 1995. "Moral Hazard, Financial Constraints, and Share Cropping in El Oulja." *Review of Economic Studies* **62**:3, 381–99.

Levine, David K. 1998. "Modeling Altruism and Spitefulness in Experiments." *Review of Economic Dynamics* **1**:3, 593–622.

Lim, C. 1984. *Economic Structuring in Singapore*. Singapore: Federal Publications.

Loewenstein, George F., Leigh Thompson, and Max H. Bazerman. 1989. "Social Utility and Decision Making in Interpersonal Contexts." *Journal of Personality and Social Psychology* **57**:3, 426–41.

Luttmer, Erzo F. P. 2001. "Group Loyalty and the Taste for Redistribution." *Journal of Political Economy* **109**:3, 500–28.

Mesa-Lago, C. 1989. "Costa Rica: A Latecomer Turned Boomer," in *Ascent to Bankruptcy: Financing Social Security in Latin America*. C. Mesa-Lago ed. University of Pittsburgh Press.

Meyer, Jack. 1987. "Two Moment Decision Models and Expected Utility." *American Economic Review* **77**:3, 421–30.

Miller, D. 1999. *Principles of Social Justice*. Cambridge, MA: Harvard University Press.

Moene, K. O. 1998. "Feasibility of Social Democracy." *Conference on Decentralised Development*, Calcutta: University of Oslo.

Moene, K. O. and M. Wallerstein. 1993. "The Decline of Social Democracy," in *The Economic Development of Denmark and Norway since 1879*. K. G. Persson ed. Gloucester: Edward Elgar.

    1995a. "How Social Democracy Worked: Labor-Market Institutions." *Politics and Society* **23**, 185–212.

    1995b. "Solidaristic Wage Bargaining." *Nordic Journal of Political Economy* **22**, 79–94.

Moffitt, R., D. Ribar, and M. Wilhelm. 1998. "Decline of Welfare Benefits in the US: the Role of Wage Inequality." *Journal of Public Economics* **68**:3, 421–52.

Moore, Barrington Jr. 1978. *Injustice: The Social Bases of Obedience and Revolt*. White Plains: M. E. Sharpe.

Oh, Seung-yun, Yong-jin Park, and Samuel Bowles. 2012. "Veblen Effects, Political Representation and the 20th-Century Decline in Working Time." Requested revision under review at *Journal of Economic Behavior and Organization*.

Okun, Arthur. 1975. *Equality and Efficiency: The Big Trade-Off*. Washington, DC: Brookings Institution Press.

Olson, Mancur. 1965. *The Logic of Collective Action: Public Goods and the Theory of Groups*. Cambridge, MA: Harvard University Press.

Ostrom, Elinor, James Walker, and Roy Gardner. 1992. "Covenants with and without a Sword: Self-Governance is Possible." *American Political Science Review* **86**:2, 404–17.

Pagano, Ugo. 1991. "Property Rights, Asset Specificity, and the Division of Labour under Alternative Capitalist Relations." *Cambridge Journal of Economics* **15**:3, 315–42.

    1993. "Organizational Equilibria and Institutional Stability," in *Markets and Democracy: Participation, Accountability and*

Efficiency. S. Bowles, H. Gintis, and B. Gustafsson eds. Cambridge University Press.

2001. "The Origin of Organizational Species," in *The Evolution of Economic Diversity*. Ugo Pagano and Antonio Nicita eds. London: Routledge.

Parijs, Philippe van. 1995. *Real Freedom for All: What (If Anything) Can Justify Capitalism?* Cambridge University Press.

Persson, Torsten and Guido Tabellini. 1996. "Is Inequality Harmful for Growth? Theory and Evidence." *American Economic Review* **48**, 600–21.

Phelps, Edmund S. 1997. *Rewarding Work: How to Restore Participation and Self-Support to Free Enterprise*. Cambridge, MA: Harvard University Press.

Phillips, Peter and Martin Brown. 1986. "The Historical Origin of Job Ladders in the US Canning Industry and their Effects on the Gender Division of Labour." *Cambridge Journal of Economics* **10**, 129–45.

Piketty, Thomas. 1995. "Social Mobility and Redistributive Politics." *Quarterly Journal of Economics*, **770**:3, 551–84.

Putzel, J. nd. "The Politics of Agrarian Reform in South Korea." London School of Economics.

Rabin, Matthew. 1993. "Incorporating Fairness into Game Theory and Economics." *American Economic Review* **83**:5, 1281–302.

Ramachandran, V. K. 1996. "On Kerala's Development Achievements," in *Indian Development: Selected Regional Perspectives*. J. Dreze and A. Sen eds. Oxford University Press.

Ransom, Roger L. and Richard Sutch. 1977. *One Kind of Freedom: The Economic Consequences of Emancipation*. Cambridge University Press.

Reif, K. and A. Melich. 1993. "Euro-Barometer 31A: European Elections, 1989: Post-Election Survey, June–July 1989" [computer file]. Conducted by Faits et Opinions, Paris. ICPSR ed. Ann Arbor, MI: Inter-university Consortium for Political and Social Research (producer and distributor).

Roberts, K. 1977. "Voting Over Income Schedules." *Journal of Public Economics* **8**, 329–40.

Rodrik, Dani. 1998. "Why Do Open Economies Have Larger Governments." *Journal of Political Economy* **106**.

Roemer, John. 1993. "A Pragmatic Theory of Responsibility for the Egalitarian Planner." *Philosophy and Public Affairs* **22**, 146–66.

1996. *Equal Shares: Making Market Socialism Work.* London: Verso.

Rosenberg, M. 1981. "Social Reform in Costa Rica: Social Security and the Presidency of Rafael Angel Calderon." *Hispanic American Historical Review* **61**:2, 278–96.

Rosenzweig, Mark and Hans P. Binswanger. 1993. "Wealth, Weather Risk and the Composition and Profitability of Agricultural Investments." *Economic Journal* **103**:416, 56–78.

Rosenzweig, Mark and Kenneth I. Wolpin. 1993. "Credit Market Constraints, Consumption Smoothing, and the Accumulation of Durable Production Assets in Low-Income Countries: Investment in Bullocks in India." *Journal of Political Economy* **101**:2, 223–44.

Saha, Atanu, Richard C. Shumway, and Hovav Talpaz. 1994. "Joint Estimation of Risk Preference Structure and Technology Using Expo-Power Utility." *American Journal of Agricultural Economics* **76**:2, 173–84.

Savage, Howard. 1999. "Who Could Afford to Buy a House in 1995" 1–6. Washington, DC: US Census Bureau.

Scott, James C. 1976. *The Moral Economy of the Peasant: Rebellion and Subsistence in Southeast Asia.* New Haven: Yale University Press.

Sen, Amartya. 1999. *Development as Freedom.* Oxford University Press.

Sengupta, S. and H. Gazdar. 1996. "Agrarian Politics and Rural Development in West Bengal," in *Indian Development: Selected Regional Perspectives.* J. Dreze and A. Sen eds. Oxford University Press.

Shapiro, Carl and Joseph Stiglitz. 1984. "Unemployment as a Worker Discipline Device." *American Economic Review* **74**:3, 433–44.

Shiller, Robert J. 1993. *Macro Markets: Creating Institutions for Managing Society's Largest Economic Risks.* Oxford: Clarendon Press.

Sinn, H. W. 1990. "Expected Utility, mu-sigma Preferences, and Linear Distribution Classes: A Further Result." *Journal of Risk and Uncertainty* **3**, 277–81.

1995. "A Theory of the Welfare State." *Scandinavian Journal of Economics* **95**:4, 495–526.

1997. "The Selection Principle and Market Failure in Systems Competition." *Journal of Public Economics* **66**, 247–74.

Stiglitz, Joseph. 1987. "The Causes and Consequences of the Dependence of Quality on Price." *Journal of Economic Literature* **25**:1, 1–48.

Taylor, A. 1999. "International Capital Mobility in History." Working paper. Cambridge, MA: National Bureau of Economic Research.

Trivers, R. L. 1971. "The Evolution of Reciprocal Altruism." *Quarterly Review of Biology* **46**, 35–57.

van Parijs, Philippe and Robert van der Veen. 1986. "A Capitalist Road to Communism." *Theory and Society*, **15**, 635–55.

Vega, Sara. 1999. "Short-Term Lending Final Report." Illinois Department of Financial Institutions.

Verba, Sidney, Kay Lehman Schlozman, and Henry Brady. 1995. *Voice and Equality: Civic Voluntarism in American Politics*. Cambridge, MA: Harvard University Press.

Weber, Eugen. 1976. *Peasants into Frenchmen: The Modernization of Rural France, 1870–1914*. Stanford University Press.

Williamson, J. B. 1974. "Beliefs about the Motivation of the Poor and Attitudes Toward Poverty Policy." *Social Problems* **21**:5, 734–47.

Wood, Elisabeth. 2003. *Insurgent Collective Action and Civil War in El Salvador*. Cambridge University Press.

World Bank. 2011. *World Development Indicators*. Washington, DC: The World Bank.

Wright, Erik Olin. 2010. *Envisioning Real Utopias*. London: Verso.

Yager, J. 1980. *Transforming Agriculture in Taiwan: The Experience of the Joint Commission on Rural Reconstruction*. Ithaca and London: Cornell University Press.

Yang, M. 1970. *Socioeconomic Results of Land Reform in Taiwan*. Honolulu: East-West Center Press.

Yashar, D. J. 1995. "Civil War and Social Welfare: The Origins of Costa Rica's Competitive Party System," in *Building Democratic Institutions: Party Systems in Latin America*. S. Mainwaring and T. Scully eds. Stanford University Press.

Yitzhaki, Shlomo. 1987. "On The Relation Between Return and Income." *Quarterly Journal of Economics* **102**:1, 77–95.

Index

184